Last Night's fun

Belfast Confetti

The Irish for No

First Language

The New Estate and Other Poems

Opera et Cetera

Last Night's fun

IN AND OUT OF TIME WITH IRISH MUSIC

Ciaran Carson

North Point Press

FARRAR, STRAUS AND GIROUX · NEW YORK

For

Deirdre Shannon,
who was with it all the way

Library of Congress Cataloging-in-Publication Data

Carson, Ciarán, 1948–
    Last night's fun : in and out of time with Irish music/Ciarán
Carson.
        p.   cm.
    ISBN 0-86547-511-3 (alk. paper)
    1. Folk music—Ireland—History and criticism.   I. Title.
ML3654.C38 1997
781.62´9162´009—dc20   96-35329

You know, there's an awful lot to be said
for this Irish traditional
folk music and folklore, because
first of all
you have to learn it
and first you must learn the Talk
and then you must learn the Grip
and after that you must learn the Truckly-How
and then
you have the whole lot
only just to keep on practising it.

Because
Séamus Ennis knows far more about this
than even the old Folk Lordy-Lordy themselves.
Because Séamus Ennis
once met a little Leprashoneen Truckly-How
at the bottom of the Garden Doth and up the Garden Path
which came up from that,
in the Limeretti-Lumeretti Hillhockers,
before the Earthian Throe,
before the Leprashonerian –
long before the Argay Foray –
and that was in the Deep Pond Doom
before the Emerald Isle was dropped . . .
in the water.

Séamus Ennis

Contents

Acknowledgements and Permissions

I want to thank Neil Belton, who encouraged me to write this book; also Tess Gallagher, for numerous editorial suggestions; and Nicholas Carolan for editorial suggestions and corrections of fact; also Sam Murray, Helen Brennan-Corcoran, Francis McPeake, Fintan Vallely and Len Graham.

The author and publisher are grateful for permission to reprint lines from the following:

Extracts on cheironomy from *The New Grove Dictionary of Musical Instruments*, ed. Stanley Sade, copyright © Macmillan 1984, reprinted by permission of Macmillan, London; Richard Klein, *Cigarettes are Sublime*, copyright © 1995, Duke University Press, Durham, N.C. Reprinted with permission; Story-telling of Mick Hoy taken from *Here is a Health: Songs and Music from Co. Fermanagh*, ed. Sean Corcoran, copyright © Arts Council of Northern Ireland 1986, reprinted by permission of Arts Council of Northern Ireland; *A Song for Every Season* by Bob Copper, copyright © Bob Copper 1971, reprinted by permission of William Heinemann, London; 'Ballad in Plain D' by Bob Dylan, copyright © Special Rider/Sony Music Publishing 1964, reprinted by permission of Sony Music Publishing, London; 'Street Musicians' from *The Branching Stair* by John Ash, copyright © John Ash 1984, reprinted by permission of Carcenet Press, Manchester; 'Silver Dagger' by Joan Baez, copyright © 1960 Chandos Music, California, USA. Lyric reproduction by kind permission of Carlin Music Corporation, UK administrator; Extract from *Setting Foot on the Shores of Connemara* by Tim Robinson, copyright © Tim Robinson 1984,

Last Night's Fun

We are in Ballyweird on the outskirts of Portrush, County Antrim, and it's the morning after the night before. Or rather, it is sometime after noon, and we've just staggered back from the local Spar, laden with the makings of a fry: bacon, sausages, black pudding, white pudding, potato bread (or, as we call it, fadge) and the yellow cornmeal soda farls peculiar to the north-west region. It's all sizzling in the pan. The almost-visible aroma wafts through the house. Soon, everything will be arrayed on mis-matched plates. We will contemplate it briefly before eating it: the wavy bacon and the frilly-crisp, flipped-over eggs; the puckered burst seams of the sausages; the milk-tooth bits of fat in the black pudding. It all glistens under a glaze of melted lard, ornamented by the fadge and soda cut in neat triangles. Tendrils of steam rise from the six odd cups. No words are spoken as we ruminate and gulp. Then plates are pushed away, cigarettes lit.

Through the haze some fragments of the night before come back: we leaned into the horizontal rain and starry dark that blows in from the cliffs, encumbered by our soaking greatcoats, our flutes and pipes and fiddles and our carry-outs. Our shadows loomed and dwindled in the lights of desultory traffic. We were coming from The Harbour Bar, from the cramped empty back lounge where we'd started to play in the early evening, that later became claustrophobic, everyone squeezed into corners, with barely elbow-room for fiddle-bow or flute, though someone has elbowed up to the TV-sized serving-hatch and is trying to order a round. Was there a serving-hatch? I'm trying to remember. I do remember standing at the mahogany counter of the bar itself, possibly as a respite from the goings-on in the so-called lounge, or maybe as a prelude to them. I stood there many times, trying to remember when I'd been there last. I contemplate the glinting rows of bottles in the carved ornate reredos. Coleraine. Power's. Bushmills, and a curious defunct whiskey whose name I don't remember, but which was labelled 'Irish Scotch'. I have ordered a nip of it just to taste, when a tune drifts out from the back: they're playing 'Last Night's Fun' again. Or maybe it is we who are playing it, the night before the morning after, before we left to spend the early hours and see the dawn in Ballyweird. I think it's 1979.

The first time I heard 'Last Night's Fun' (no, rather, the first time I knew it *was* 'Last Night's Fun' that I was listening to, for I must have heard it many times before without knowing its name, or knowing the tune itself, for that matter), was from a record of the accordion-player, the late Joe Cooley. Entitled simply, *Cooley*, the album was produced in 1975 by the accordion-player Tony MacMahon, who adopted and adapted the Cooley style to make his own music.

The recording is done in mono, and has that lively, crackly, jumpy feel of the old 78s, the kind of noise anathematic to the CD generation – and here I remember reading a pronouncement of the maestro Karajan, heralding the new technology in whatever year it was, that before CD, 'everything was gaslight'; well, what's wrong with gaslight? For you can use your imagination, make figures out of shadow. And lo-fi has a beauty and a logic all of its own, which has something to do with the imperfectibility of listening or hearing, or of the act of recording itself. Where do you put the mikes? What are you looking for? In any session of music, no one will hear the same thing: it will depend on context, on placement, on experience – whether or not you've heard the tune before, whether or not the person next to you knows the tune that you might only half-know.

But do we ever fully *know* a tune, or only versions of it, temporary delineations of the possible? The boy sitting at one end of a row of five or six musicians will not perceive the tune the same as someone at the other end. Bar acoustics are peculiar. Wooden floors resound and carpets muffle. One hot-water geyser, unbeknownst to itself, will mimic the tenor drone of a barely-tuned set of pipes. The rhythmic rattling of loose change in punters' trouser-pockets has lost its plangency since decimal coinage came in. And the sound of an accordion played by someone with his coat on is different when that same someone takes off his coat.

So back to Cooley. As Tony MacMahon describes it:

November 29, 1973, was a wet dreary Thursday, but Lahiff's bar in the village of Peterswell was thronged. Gathered from the nooks and corners of counties Clare and Galway were old friends of Cooley – people who had followed the wild call of his music through many a night down the years. They felt in their hearts that this was to be the last great blast of *ceol* with Joe. . . In an atmosphere charged with excitement, and the sorrow just under the surface, Cooley played for his friends, while those who couldn't get in pressed their faces to the dripping November window panes. His brother Jack played the *bodhrán* with him, and Des Mulkere the banjo.

What follows, on Side One, is one of the best recordings of Irish traditional music ever made. The accordion is – as is its wont – slightly out of tune in the top register; and Des Mulkere's banjo is maybe not perfect either, and the *bodhrán* . . . Box, banjo, *bodhrán*, an unlikely combination: it doesn't matter. The plectral gunky sound of the banjo is just right for the business in hand. The supporting drum weaves in the beat and off-beat; what matters is the melody, the beat; Joe's drawing out the wild notes in places, making little deft chromatic runs in others – bits and bytes and phrases constantly negotiated and re-arranged in what MacMahon calls 'the forceful logic which always seemed to run through his music'. And the place is jumping: whoops and gulders, clicking bottles, tapping feet. The whole room pulses like a diaphragm, and you can almost see the punters hunched in gleeful shapes at the bar, nodding joyfully into their pints; for though this is mono, you can hear or see in stereo, as if you were some fly-on-the-wall, disembodied lucid dreamer, some ghost from the future, floating in on the sound waves that connect the present here-and-now to the present then, some twenty years ago. And in the lull between tunes, a few poignant bits of talk from Joe. The voice is grainy, smoky, hesitant:

'It's the only music that brings people to their senses, I think . . .'

'America is a very big place . . . but I think I was in most towns in it, anyway . . . Philadelphia, Chicago I was . . .'

and

'A lot of people all over Ireland thought I was dead . . . a couple of times . . . but . . . so . . . my voice is not as good as it used to be . . .'

Then Side Two, which brings us further back in time, to 1963, where Joe meets up with Joe Leary, the fiddle-player. He and Leary travelled Clare and Galway in the early Fifties, 'travelling dusty, icy or rainy roads on a motorcycle, the fiddle slung over Cooley's back, the accordion tied to the fuel tank'. The broadcaster Ciarán Mac Mathúna has gathered them together in the piano-player Bridie Lafferty's front room in Home Farm Road in Dublin. They play 'The Skylark', 'Roaring Mary' and 'My Love is in America'. Then further back again, we are in Chicago, 1962. Joe is playing with a *ceili* band. Again, the place is jumping; Joe is in full flight on 'The Ships are Sailing', soaring above the cacophonous drums and the hum and buzz and clatter of the dance floor. We catch a snippet of conversation just off-mike, or just-on, a girl's Galway accent going, 'I haven't seen him dancing in years'. You have to put your ear to the speaker again and again, rewinding and pressing 'play' over and over just to get the fragment, this isolated phrase in time. Who was he? Who was she? And did he ever dance again?

So to the last tune, 'The Sailor on the Rock', played with Des Mulkere in July 1972 in Galway. 'When you play this track,' says Tony MacMahon, 'listen between the notes for the great heart that was in this man's music.' So you do, again and again, hearing something different every time, trying to remember what you heard the last time, trying to relive those moments, not knowing what you'll hear in the future.

Joe Cooley died of lung cancer on 21 December 1973.

I turn over the sleeve. The sleeve is Cooley's face and shoulders and the upper half of the box, the straps digging into his collar-bone, the Paolo Soprani radiator-grille Art Deco aluminium sound-plate-and-fingerboard on his right, the bellows on his left stretched in an elegant accordioned ridge. He has his jacket on. A floppy-collared shirt, a tie; a jaunty cigarette between his lips. It is a gaslight snap, blown up till all the grains show, till you are drawn in to reinvent the smile you imagine to be there behind the eyes in shadow, as you are drawn into the gas of the recording, of the mono LP hissing blackly and revolving in its shellacky crepuscular upon the turntable of an archaic Decca mahogany-veneered radiogram the size of a china cabinet, with its dog-sized speakers and dead mice inside them, after you foolishly abandoned them in the back room of the damp mouse-infested gardener's cottage that you left for where you live now. I'm back there now, and Joe is playing 'Last Night's Fun'.

Ask My Father

'Last Night's Fun', to take an example, is a name or a label for a tune: it does not describe its musical activity nor impute experience to it. It is not *about* frolics revelled in on some particular night, although the name might put you in mind of them. In other words, the tune, by any other name, would sound as sweet; or as rough, for that matter, depending on who plays it, or what shape they're in.

So, the names of tunes are *not* the tunes: they are tags, referents, snippets of speech which find themselves attached to musical encounters. Some come from happenstance and gabble: 'I Do Not Incline'; 'One Bottle More'; 'Sorry, Too Late'. Of course there are the usual exceptions to this rule: pieces like 'The Hen's March O'er the Midden' or 'The Fox-chase', where there is a supposed relationship between the music and the sounds of hens, foxes, dogs, hunting horns and the like. These arrangements are thankfully rare; but the notion persists in certain quarters that the names mean what they say, and that the tunes attached to them are a representation of some occurrence in the natural world. A Barbara Callaghan, writing in *Treoir* * (the official organ of the Irish Musicians' Association, Comhaltas Ceoltóirí Éireann) complains that although many musicians can recall exactly where they learned the tune, how long ago, and from whom, they often don't have a name for it. She goes on:

> So much can be obtained from the very title alone. Take 'The Lark in the Morning', for instance. Close your eyes and imagine the morning air, cool and refreshing. The lark waking early to greet the day. The first part of the tune, where she raises her sleepy head from the nest, isn't quite so exciting as the second

* *Treoir*, Vol. 10, 1978, No. 6

part when I like to feel that she is wheeling and gliding about on the wind, perhaps hunting the proverbial worm. The third part to me is self-explanatory. She is so obviously taking her bath in sandy soil or water, shaking and ruffling her feathers. Good control of volume here produces a really dramatic effect and brings you to the fourth part which is alive and busy with activity. A real story within a tune, and the plot begins to unfold with the title. How sad if such an air became known by the title 'Don't Know'.

Well, I don't know. For a start, Ms Callaghan's referring to the tune as an 'air' leads one to suspect that she is not a traditional musician, since *tune* always refers to a dance tune as distinct from a song air which will be attached to words. A song might have a narrative; a dance tune does not. The lark's bath-water is further muddied given the fact that O'Neill's *Music of Ireland* offers two distinct settings of a two-part jig called 'The Lark in the Morning', neither of which bears any resemblance to the four-part tune known to some by the same name; and I was once rebuked by the great Séamus Ennis for referrring to it as 'The Lark in the Morning' – I believe he called it 'The Lark's March'. Our suspicions deepen further when we find that Ms Callaghan believes that 'some incidence inspired the composer to map out dots on the stave for posterity, and who are we to ignore this?' For tunes are not dots on a stave: more of this anon.

At any rate, the tune is not a story, but stories might lie behind the tune. For, as mnemonics, the names summon up a tangled web of circumstances; they not only help to summon the tune into being, but recall other times and other places where the tune was played, and the company there might have been. The same tune – or what is recognised by some as being the same, for others might disagree – might have many names. 'Rolling in the Rye-grass', according to Breandán Breathnach's *Ceol Rince na hÉireann*, is known also as 'Maureen Playboy', 'Old Molly Ahern', 'The Piper's Lass', 'The Rathkeale Hunt', 'The Shannon Breeze', 'The Lady's Top Dress', 'The Lady's Tight Dress', 'The Telegraph', 'What the Divil Ails Him?', 'Roll Her on the Banks', 'The Railway Station', 'The Connachtman's Rambles', 'McCaffrey's Reel', 'What the Devil Ails You?', 'The Lady on the Railroad', 'The Brown Red Girl', 'Love Among the Roses', 'The Kilfinane Reel', 'The Listowel

Lasses', 'Boil the Kettle Early', 'Kitty Got a Clinking' (also the name of a completely different reel) and 'Punch for the Ladies'.

In their metamorphoses and *non sequiturs*, in their slips of the tongue, in their Chinese Whispers, in their curious accretions of proper and improper names, the titles of this tune might form a story-board for some hybrid of Somerville & Ross and *film noir*, an alternative universe whose underlying principles are steam and gender. The tune is an annex of the omnivorous world described by Breandán Breathnach in his diverting bagatelle of an essay, 'The Nomenclature of Irish Dance Music' (printed in *Sinsear*, 1981), which sparked off this long gloss of mine, where:

> Clothing was a mixed bag. Bonnets and caps including night caps were worn. A mason's apron perhaps is not admissable here but knee-breeches, breeks and frieze breeches are as well as flannel jackets and green jerseys. Pants, petticoats, tight and loose, pantalettes and pantaloons with skirts and shirts and shifts complete our list. Accessories included buttons, ribbons, garters, earrings and gold rings. Calico, frieze, flannel (usually flannin) and silk were seemingly the only fabrics in use.
>
> An air of gaiety pervaded the community. Old and new were equally favoured. Green was the most popular colour but orange and yellow too were in vogue as well as black and white and brown. Sporting, merry and jolly were in equal use to describe boon companions who gave vent to their vagaries whenever the whim, fancy or maggot seized them.

There are, as Breathnach suggested, patterns and systems to be glimpsed in 'the nomenclature', and here some definitions from the *Shorter Oxford English Dictionary* seem germane: 'a glossary, a vocabulary; the system or set of names for things, etc., commonly employed by a person or community; the terminology of a science'. An example given is 'He rank't in the N. of fools' – which brings to mind, incidentally, the many Ulster dialect forms of such: *geck, glipe, ganch, gulpin, gommeril* (to name a few), each having their own stance and accent in the hierarchy and their own peculiar foolish things to do. These are fine distinctions, just as there are between tunes. Breathnach comments:

Some interesting patterns come to light in the grouping of place names and the human categories. Boys and girls as well as maids invariably precede the place name; lasses always follow it. 'The Boys of the Lough', of Ballisodare and of Ballinamore, 'The Girls of Banbridge', of Ballaugh and of 'Our Town' with 'The Maids of Mitchelstown', of Carrick and of Ballincarty illustrate the first usage. 'The Fermoy Lasses' immediately comes to mind in the second case. Clonmel, Dublin, Limerick, Listowel and London can also be mentioned here. All reels, be it noted, so some temporal cause may underline this usage.

Taking it that 'temporal cause' refers to musical and not historical time, there would appear to be rhythmic distinctions between the two usages; but running the permutations through my head – how these split hairs might apply to the first or last bar of a tune, for instance – it is difficult to form a constant law. So it should be. The names hint at some deep structure replete with corrigenda and addenda, but still remain elusive. Where tunes are concerned, there is no final version. The notion of correctness is anathema.

Persons who are in the habit of referring Irish music to 'composers' insist very strongly on having what they call correct versions. They seem to think that there is an absolutely fixed setting which pre-eminently holds the palm beyond all others. They are helped to this notion by seeing Irish airs and dance music printed, as, for instance, 'Patrick's Day' or 'The Girl I Left Behind Me'. But such a condition of things was absolutely unknown to Irish or to any folk music. Why, as a matter of fact, no two stanzas of any Irish song have exactly the same music, for that must yield to the words, and if the music persists the same throughout the song it is an infallible sign that it is not the work of a traditional singer. In fact, this very changing constitutes a main ornament and beauty of Irish singing. The same rule was observed in playing dance music, for all the good players introduced similar changes every time the tune came round, and the musician who could not play in that style was not regarded as a master. And as to versions of dancing tunes, it may be useful to explain that whenever a musician heard a note or an accent change in a tune that he considered an improvement, he straightway incorporated it in his own version. I particularly remember in my own case, as a boy, how, on fair days and other occasions of visiting towns, I used to listen with the closest attention to such tramp pipers or fiddlers as I chanced to hear, especially if their style was good or they happened to be playing any of the great reels or other dance tunes, in order to assimilate for myself such changes of version or interpretation as I considered suitable. And I never knew an Irish musician who did not do the same. Now, if this system of election has always and universally been going on, as it certainly was, and not only in instrumental music, but in singing also, then who shall say what is the absolute version of a given tune, for such a thing clearly does not and never did exist.

That was the Revd Dr Richard Henebry, writing in his brilliant, eccentric and sometimes opaque *A Handbook of Irish Music* (1928). I have assimilated or incorporated his words here as illustration of his thesis.

It is possible, of course, to 'learn' a tune from the page, from what is there in black and white, but this requires negotiation and imagination. It requires you to know that what is written is a mere mnemonic, not an actual performance (it is impossible to transcribe an actual performance), nor the dynamic pulse of what it can be when it's played and heard and danced. You have to go by your experience of other tunes which seem to have the same shape, and to perceive when this particular tune is different, and the value of that difference. You also have to contemplate the possibility that a tune's notation may be written 'wrongly' – 'wrong', here, meaning out of character or sympathy with the genre. For while there is no ultimate correctness in traditional music, there is wrong: the attempts of such as Yehudi Menuhin or James Galway to play 'simple' Irish hornpipes, for example. Such interpretations are simplistic and one-dimensional – they ignore the possibilities. They take the tune as read whilst a traditional musician plays the tune as heard.

One of the beauties of traditional playing is the way a good musician can produce a pulse against the ostensible rhythm of the tune. The result is a kind of *double entendre* – like hearing two beats at once – and it is appropriate that many tune titles are on the verge of *double entendre*, or maybe oxymoron: 'The Active Old Man', 'The Funny Mistake', 'Good Morning to Your Nightcap'. 'Moll Halfpenny' is possibly a deliberate garbling of 'Poll Ha'penny', which might be a version of the English tune 'Holey Ha'penny' (*poll* being Irish for hole), and it probably belongs to that class of title which includes 'The Maid at the Fair', 'Pay the Girl her Fourpence' and 'The Two-and-Sixpenny Girl' (also known as 'The Money I Want' and 'The Spirits of Whiskey'). 'Jennie Bang the Weaver' is, in Scotland, 'Jenny Dang the Weaver'. Ostensibly more up-market, 'The Duke of Leinster's Wife' is alternatively called 'The Lady's Pantalettes', while in a coarser vein, 'O'Farrell's Welcome to Limerick' is, in Irish, '*An Phis Fhliuch*'.

Sometimes the *entendre* is *non sequitur*; or maybe it is a triple-, or a double-take. I remember being at a musical weekend in Derrygonnelly, County Fermanagh, where this exchange took place between the fiddle-player Mick Hoy and the concertina-player Gabriel McArdle (Mick has just played a tune relatively unfamiliar to Gabriel):

G: And what do you call that tune, Mick?
M: They call it 'The Black Rogue', Gaby.
G: 'The Black Rogue'?
M: And *you* call it 'The Black Rogue', Gaby?

Gaby looked nonplussed.

'The Black Rogue' reminds me that I once met, in Brittany, a group called *Sonerien Du* (The Black Musicianers) whose name came from a pair of boys at the turn of the century well known for japes and pranks. And there is a prankishness, a funny, Zen-like sidelong way of seeing things in many titles: 'Though Late I was Plump', 'Tell Her I Am', 'Upstairs in a Tent', 'The Humours of Flip', 'It Goes as Follies', 'Funny Eye', 'The Dear Meal', 'Are You Shot?', 'Cornelius Curtin's Big Balloon' (deflated, slightly, when you know that Con Curtin runs a pub in London called 'The Balloon').

And then there is the important category touched on by Ms Callaghan: the 'Anons.' of the musical nomenclature, tunes with no names – in Irish, *Gan Ainm* (without name), or, as is frequently written, sometimes by those who should know better, *Gan Anam* (without soul). But of course namelessness is no bar to playing these orphans (there is a jig, 'The Orphan', a version or a child of 'The Star of the County Down'). There are codes for mentioning the unmentionable.

A pub session: someone has just played a bar of a tune:

A: What do you call that?
B: I don't know.
C: Ah . . .
D: No, I don't know either.
B: I'll tell you what, we'll play that one anyway . . .
C: And then we'll play the other one after it, you know, the one we used to play before it.
ALL: Right!

They launch into 'The Tune', and then, 'The One After It'. Or maybe it's the other way round.
Another session:

A: What do you call that?
B: Ask my father.
A: 'Ask My Father'?

Was A a novice? Or a prankster? Who can tell?

Or, two musicians are cutting turf. A asks the other, B, for a
reel he half
Remembers. The other takes his spade. In the bank of turf he
cuts a staff.
Then the notes. O'Keefe was one of them. I think the other was
a Murph.
Of course the notes are not the tune. The tune itself they called
'The Bank of Turf'.

Boil the Breakfast Early

The science or the art of cooking has a nomenclature as complicated as any. If traditional musicians are engaged with constant repetition and renewal, infinite fine-tunings and shades of rhythms, variations on the basic, cooks are even more so. The *Larousse Gastronomique* lists some two hundred and ninety recipes for eggs alone, and this is not even counting the various omelettes.

'He couldn't even boil an egg' – this from someone who seemingly has no experience of the matter in hand, because it all depends. The freshness of the egg, the weather, the altitude, the water, whether you add salt or not, and whether you start from cold or boiling: all these are important factors in what seems a simple operation. If two eggs are boiled at once, the first one might be perfect; the second, by the time you come to it, will be overdone (we will not enter here into the relative merits of bashing the cranium of the egg with a spoon or of slicing it open). I like a firm white and a viscous-liquid yolk. Others like a fairly hard-boiled egg smashed up in a cup with lots of butter, salt and pepper. Others like theirs nearly raw, as the piper Francis McPeake tells it:

> *So there we were, the McPeake Family,*
> *over in London for the big do,*
> *this big Folk Festival they had that time.*
> *And there was all sorts of folk*
> *from different parts,*
> *all dressed up in their national costumes.*
> *And there we were, just*
> *in our working clothes and cloth caps.*
> *And anyway, we were in the Albert Hall*

and we've been playing for a while,
it's going right and well.
And my Daddy leans over to me
and he says, Francie,
do you think we'll let them hear
'Will You Go Lassie, Go'?
And I says, Daddy, fire away.
So we do 'Will You Go Lassie, Go'
and it went down great.
It was that good, there was like about
a minute's silence
before they burst into applause.

So the next morning – we're stopping
at this big hotel in London,
and we're at our breakfast.
And there's a queue of journalists
a mile long at the door,
waiting for to interview my Daddy,
to ask him how he sang that well.
And he says, boys, hold your horses.
Now you know,
according to my Daddy,
there wasn't a chef in the whole of London
could boil an egg right.
So he says to the waiter, he says,
go out to the kitchen
and bring me an egg
and a pan of boiling water.
So the waiter brings the egg and water.
And my Daddy takes the egg
and he puts it into the water.
He takes out his watch
and he times two minutes.
The he takes the egg out
and he puts it in the egg-cup.
He takes a knife.
He slices off the top.

Then, OK, boys, he says,
yez can come in now.
And the first boy has his notebook out,
his pencil, and he says,
Mr McPeake, he says, where did you get it from,
the way you sang that song so well
last night?
So my Daddy lifts the egg
out from the egg-cup, with his thumb and finger,
like it was a glass of spirits
and he puts it to his lips, and
slu-r-r-r-r-p, he goes,
and swallows it, and says, that's
where I got it from.

Then there is the fried egg, which has its own vocabulary. Like many others, I recall the first time I ordered bacon and eggs in a New York diner:

A: How do you want your eggs?
B: Well . . . fried, I suppose.
A: What do you mean, fried? You want basted, over-easy, sunny-side-up, over-hard, or what?

'Sunny-side-up' sounded attractive, and I'd heard them being ordered in American films. When they came, they weren't what I'd wanted: they were too wobbly. Now I know, having been there some more times, that 'over-easy' is the answer. With whole-wheat toast. I haven't, as yet, been able to bring myself to try the grape jelly that they give you without asking, but I love their thick white delph coffee cups and their inexhaustible free coffee, their fluted-glass sugar dispensers, their orange juice with bits in it, their different bacon, their link sausages.

Even the Irish fried egg has many schools of thought, its many factions. I remember some time in the late Seventies or early Eighties being at a *fleadh* in Ballycastle, and we are debating, Deirdre Shannon, Tommy Sands, Mote Mullen (called Mote because there was this other older Mullen called Mote, and they called him after him) and me, the best way to fry an egg. It is that sort of idle conversation that arises when the pubs are closed and you're hanging around waiting for a rumour of the after-hours crack, and the consistency of an egg suddenly takes on a Scrabble-like importance. Mote is a crispy-edged man, who likes the oil (or, preferably, lard) to come to that blue-haze shimmering point of heat when the egg spits and frizzles as you drop it in; then you break the yolk up with your fried-egg implement, your spatula, whatever, and you flip it over when the underside is hard, and you press it down into the lard until the edges are just slightly burnt and crispy, like fried lace. Tommy is a basted man: medium heat; tip the pan over to one side when the egg has set a little; then you get a big dessert spoon and you scoop the oil and dribble it all over the egg, till the yolk takes on a golden glazed veil. Deirdre's over-medium-hard, with a slightly liquid centre.

Then we engage the wider lexicon of 'The Fry', where the possibilities become Byzantine. Some exclude fried mushrooms or potatoes, say, from their definition of The Fry, as being side issues – distractions from the business in hand. Others, in their catholicity, include fried apples, or *bananas*, which to me is another version of the American aberrant grape jelly. And sometimes I am attracted to a Puritan ideal of bacon and eggs, nothing more, nothing less. For The Fry can be an immense orchestration of diverse but related materials.

Take the various breads, for example: soda farls, wheaten farls, pancakes, crumpets, potato bread, potato cakes, oven wheaten, pan loaf, plain loaf; then, how they are modified by how they're cut, and whether they are fried or not, and which should be fried on both sides. These breads alone form complex permutations of etiquette and taste whose demarcations are eternally disputed and perused. In Northern Ireland or the North of Ireland, whatever it is called, according to the company you keep, these breads are the base or the ground bass around which The Fry is composed. It should be noted that this Great Northern Fry – I hesitate to call it an *Ulster Fry*, though it is advertised as such in eating-houses – comes, almost invariably, with one egg; there simply isn't room on the plate for two.

The sausage is another talking-point. Personally, I am not offended by the standard, supermarket-bought, cling-wrapped pork sausauge; others will have nothing but a butcher's sausage, but there are as many sausages as there are butchers; more, in fact, since each butcher produces a range of sausages. Here, I note the recent decadence of garlic sausages and leek-and-sun-dried-tomato things – good enough, perhaps, to be eaten on their own, but anathema to The Fry. And white pudding, if it's right – herby, with a peppery bready crumbly creamed-potato texture – is a great contrast to the thick ox-blood-black dense black pudding and its little rice-grain bits of fat and rice.

It was around this time of the great Talmudic Fry debates that Deirdre Shannon and I were playing my version of 'The Kylebrack Rambler' – a rather majestic three-part fiddle or accordion tune that went down to the bottom G, a note you can't get on the flute, so I took it up a fifth and cut out the tricky variations in the third part. In other words, I bastardised it, as I can see now; back then, I thought it worked. The old ways are often the best. And yet, it now occurs to me that it could be a far-out cousin of 'The Galway Rambler'. Bits of common structures are apparent in the scaffolding and there is no other Rambler in the nomenclature, as far as I know, so this might suggest a common origin.

'The Galway Rambler' is a straightforward, jumpy, no-prisoners-taken flute tune; 'The Kylebrack' (it's interesting that it's known also by this shortened tag) is comparatively ornate and stately, with its mock-baroque façade. It's as if the Kylebrack people wanted to upstage their distant Galway cousins, and looked down their fiddle-players' noses at these dog-rough fluters. I used to swear 'The Kylebrack' put me in mind of The Kylebrack Cafe on O'Connell Street at the corner of whatever Street it is that leads to Amiens Street Station (Connolly, they call it now) until I visited Dublin a few weeks ago and found it was really called The Kylemore; I detect a ghost of barmbrack, the fruit loaf, behind this nominal confusion.

At any rate, we'd sometimes go there on the way to catch the Belfast train. After a night of session-crack and drinking until dawn, we'd stagger up at noon after sprawling on a sofa, or lying prostrate on a technicoloured carpet. We'd drag ourselves up and open a door to try and guess our bearings. It is a windy housing-project, a narrow mews with horse-dung in the gutter, or we have opened the back door on to Dublin Bay. We do not remember how we got here, and the tenants of the house have fled, or never were there in the first place. We should have come equipped with sextants and theodolites, instead of flutes and fiddles. Going by the sun, the flow of traffic and the elaborate passers-by, we'd find the road that got you into town – *An Lár*, as they call it in Irish:

Lár: ground, floor, threshing-floor, middle, midst, centre; *fear láir an tsúsa*, the man in the middle, as in a bed; *níor fhán lár a chuimhne agam*, it passed completely from my memory . . .

At *An Lár*, we'd disembark from the No. X bus, where X stands for oft-forgotten numbers, and pour ourselves into The Kylebrack – Kylemore, rather – for The Fry. The Kylemore fry was self-service and not quite the real thing, but it was handy, and in the storm of hunger any port will do.

Then there was the cafe you always found by accident, above a haberdashery or alterations shop. The door that led upstairs was innocent of any label or description of the premises above. You sat at the white linen-covered table, and the table-silver glinted with a sudden tang of memory; you knew you'd been here many times before. Waitresses in black stockings and little frilly caps appeared to serve you. There was a little scalloped butter-dish, silver salt and pepper cellars; toast came in a toast-rack. Beside the silver tea-pot was a jug of just-boiled water. The fry arrived on thick white wide-rimmed hot delph plates – 'Mind the plates', the waitress said, as she dished them out as if she were dealing cards. All the hands were flush: the famous Dublin Hafner sausages, the exotic salty Free State bacon, the coarse fat-spotted black pudding, the unctuous creamy texture of the white. The eggs wobbled and glistened their glazed orange yolks. Two eggs, because the Dublin fry, knowing no exotic Northern breads to fry, has room for two. This was ample compensation, faced with fresh-cut chewy oven wheaten on a doily in a basket and hot toast spread with curly salty butter.

You sat at the window above the hum and buzz of the street below. At first you gulped and chewed and then decelerated as you realised that your hunger would be perfectly assuaged. Then you could eat contemplatively, picking bits and choosing bits you thought would make an interesting ensemble. You craned your neck occasionally like some astronomer, gazing downwards at the Milky Way of interweaving passing heads. The chinking noise of cutlery and crockery cut through the muted traffic noise. You pronged the last inch of Hafner's sausage on to a tiny toast triangle that you'd custom-cut, and married it to the last remaining quarter of an egg yolk. You ate these morsels in one forkful. Then a gulp of tea. You settled back contentedly. An enormous cut-glass ashtray came from nowhere. Plates vanished, and you put your elbows on the table and lit up. The bill came in its own good time, unhurriedly. You looked with some amazement at the spiky old-fashioned Staedtler HB pencil-writing, quoting prices current in the Fifties. You paid the carbon-slip. Then you descended to the mundane busy street. Absorbed into the crowd, you let yourself be taken by its flow, and became another corpuscle in its bloodstream.

We would spread the word about this last word of an eating-house. No one ever found it, nor could we again when we determined that we would, because the universe is often stumbled on by accident, or visualised in dreams. Only when the stars concur do we arrive. We stumble through the patterns of The Kylemore and The Kylebrack and we wander through the icons of the city, touching them in well-worn reliquary places. We are on a pilgrimage, and yet we do not know it. We will not know the time until the time is ripe, and even then, it passes us in one forgetful instant. Yet bits of it remain among our archaeology, the loop comes round again, and megabytes of time swim up through one split chink of time.

We are fragile, and it is the morning after; rather, it is early afternoon, and we have settled in a dusty sunlit corner of the empty pub. Our talk is desultory till we think to play a tune, and we are all reluctant. Yet we start because we have to. And somehow, two bars into it, we sense each other's playing in the way the Zodiac arrives at planetary conjunctions, and we can do no more than play the pattern out. And though the stars, by now, are out of line with what they were two hundred years ago, we too have moved, or have been moved to know that until now we had not played this tune. We did not know its beauty, nor had we realised the marks of other hands that knew it, and had passed it on to some they hoped would eventually manage to figure out its gorgeous shape. We repeat this same tune many times, and about the twelfth or thirteenth time, we know it's time to stop, since we have gained a century in those few minutes of horology. Then we were like some watchers of the skies, or we had gazed at the Pacific for the first time, and we were silent as we contemplated time in all its mirrored constellations.

Pigtown

So there was this returned Yank
came back one year
to see his Irish cousin.
And the cousin was a pig-farmer
and the Yank farmed pigs as well, in Yankee-land.
So naturally he wanted to see the Irish cousin,
to talk pigs with him
and talk about the family,
how the cousins and the uncles all were doing
and the power of the dollar
and whatever.

So he drives up in his big hired car,
the Yank, and it's some job,
getting up the boreen,
what with all the potholes and the stone walls
scraping up against the bodywork –
but he gets there, and he gets out
and there's Paddy
leaning on the half-door,
puffing on his pipe
and waiting for him,
for he saw him coming.

So the Yank says, How ya doing, Paddy?
Fine, says Paddy,
I expect you'll want to see the pigs.
Right on, says the Yank,
I sure would like to see your feeding regime –

how you feed them –
and compare it with the ways we have back home.
He'd been away from home that long,
you see.
And Paddy says, Well, come along with me,
and if you like,
I'll feed them for you right now.
So he takes him to the pigsty
round the back –
what you might call in Yankee-land
a pigpen –
and there's six or seven pigs in there.
And there's a little orchard
maybe fifty paces down the road.
And Pat says, Piggy, piggy,
and the pigs come over to him.
And he stoops down over the pigsty wall
and puts his two arms round a pig
and lifts it out.

He carries it down the boreen
to the orchard
and lifts the pig up to an apple-tree
and holds it there
and lets it munch away
until it's had its fill.
He brings it back and puts it back into the sty.
He takes another pig
and takes it to the orchard
and he holds it up
and lets it munch away
until it's had its fill,
and so on, till he has the pigs all fed.

Now, the Yank is following him around,
all this time.
He's watching him, and scratching his head,
not knowing what to make of all this.

So he says, Well, Pat,
that sure is very interesting, and I'm sure
we ain't got nothing like it back home,
but say, Pat, don't you find it very
time-consuming?

Right enough, says Paddy,
But sure, what's time to a pig?

The Ravelled Hank of Yarn

I

Hickmann postulated that the cheironomy of Pharaonic Egypt was not a conductor's art but an educational system of melodic graphs indicated by hand signs; and his shrewd attempts at deciphering 'the writing on the air' brought to light some of the 'speaking messages' depicted on tombs of antiquity. But we do not know, as yet, whether the gesticulations of the cheironomists are meant to indicate single intervals or melodic group formulae. Much remains to be discovered . . .

In the cheironomy of Jewish chant, it should be noted that the single sign hardly ever corresponds to a single note but to a complete organism of notes; i.e., to an elaborate melodic motif; and that these motifs are never themselves defined sequentially note for note. This means that internally the aggregate of notes remains fluctuating and loose while their character as a group remains constant. This is a melodic phenomenon which is closely bound to the basic mentality of oral traditions in music where the melodic memory takes the place of the visible graphic symbol. Yet the singer, while working his way through the masses of stored melodic elements, keeps the mnemonic process in equilibrium by, on one hand, following the mainstream of constant characters and, on the other, leaving room for variants to fill in the open spaces.

II

In the 'hand-winding' system of the Irish *sean-nós*, a sympathetic listener grasps the singer's hand; or, indeed, the singer may initiate first contact, and reach out for a listener. The singer then might close his eyes, if they are open (sometimes, he might grope for someone, like a blind man) and appear to go into a trance; or his eyes, if open, might focus on some remote corner of the room, as if his gaze could penetrate the fabric, and take him to some far-off, antique happening among the stars. The two clasped hands remind one another of each other, following each other; loops and spirals accompany the melody, singer and listener are rooted static to the spot, and yet the winding unwinds like a line of music with its ups and downs, its glens and plateaux and its little melismatic avalanches. One hand prompts the other as they internalise the story of the song, or the yarn behind the song – *údár an amhráin* – deferred to in a few obeisant vocal fragments, spun out in a run of ornament, a cheironomic flourish.

III

Nearly all ancient oral traditions are surprising for this double feature of endless variety within a fixed framework. In this sense, cheironomic movements were never intended to be a rational musical notation, and their air-drawn curves are no more than casual landmarks given to the expert singer, who of course knows the general direction of his chant, especially if it is connected to a running prose text of greater dimensions.

IV

The instrumentalist's hands remember patterns and melodic structures; they finger out the relatives in tune families. Such is the character of Irish traditional music that many ostensibly distinct tunes, distinguished by separate, idiosyncratic names, might be cousins, nephews, nieces, variants or mutations of each other; and this is both a blessing and a curse. Similarities, identikits or simulacra are fundamental to the learning process; so too are dissimilarities and antonyms. Learning a new tune that reminds you of another, you have to unlearn some of the salients: that last bar, for instance, in the first part, where it forms a little rhythmic and melodic bridge to the second part; while in the other tune, it is more like a gate you walk through, and you leave it swinging open, so as you can 'access' it the next time round. Then you might forget the first tune for a while, until it comes back, maybe after many years, unsought-for and unbidden. It seems the tune recalls itself, in some absentminded lull between some other tunes, when everyone except you has put down their instruments.

V

There is one manual position which has remained alive through the millennia without a break or change of meaning: the hand covering the ear of a musician. In this case no technicality of intonation, interval or motif is intended, but rather it symbolises the status of the musician as a professional singer. In addition, its purpose is to convey his prominence among the musicians as the most exalted personality, gifted with an inspired and ecstatic disposition.

VI

Such is the bent of Irish traditional music that tunes repeat: they are played at least twice, or maybe three, four or more times; then the players generally change to another tune. Getting 'the change' is a skill; it has to be watched for, and listened for, even if the number of repeats has been determined in advance (some players can't count). If the repeats have not been predetermined, the players will use body language to communicate the change – eyes, shoulders, elbows, knees, feet and hands may be deployed. Hence, the manic widening of the flute-player's eyes at the end of the first tune the third time round, or the shaking of her head which means you play the first tune again. If not agreed in advance, it will be assumed that the second tune will be that which is normally associated with the first; that is, they will form a set, as in 'The Boys of Ballisodare' and 'The Five-Mile Chase', or 'The Sally Gardens' and 'The Sligo Maid'. But sometimes there might be two or three possibilities for the second tune in the set, or you are playing with unfamiliar musicians who have a different notion of the set. Or maybe someone is inspired to form a new set there and then, or maybe someone else is bored, and craves a new experience. On such occasions silent questions will be asked by the participants: an eyebrow raised, a finger pointing to the heart, a deferring nod in someone else's direction. Such gesticulations of the body are a language. So, too, are poker and telepathy.

VII

The original meaning of cheironomy as an art of bodily gesticulation, not confined to hands and arms as suggested by the Greek name, should be considered. The latter term was itself probably coined by taking the most striking part for the whole. It is not surprising, therefore, to find that in the Jewish tradition the head and the back as well as the hand are employed in spatial writing. Their respective functions are clearly defined. Of the three, the hand is the proper didactic medium for elementary teaching in religious schools (cheder). It should be noted that the cantillation of the Bible is not an independent piece of music, but a structural recitative whose main task is to emphasise the syntax of the individual sentences, especially to mark separation between each of them by means of an idiomatic melisma or thematic flourish. Small children learn first how to chant the syntactical motifs and how to string them together according to the ever-changing structures of the prose texts. Only when the melodic outlines are well memorised is the holy text interpolated, at a second stage of learning. Here then is the place of the didactic hand 'waving' and 'winking' (neuma) used by the teacher to indicate the general outlines of melody, and – even more so – its continuous flow and its animated spirituality (pneuma).

VIII

It is the morning after the night before, or rather, early afternoon. Its sunshine filters through an etched-glass window and lights on fiddle-cases, pints and flute-boxes. The slowly-setting pints are still untouched. Some time will pass before there is a move towards music. Then a fiddle-player, maybe, looks with feigned uncertainty at the case beside him. He takes it on his knee and snaps the catches open like you might undo a baby's Babygro. He opens up the lid and looks astonished that the fiddle is still there, as if it were a waif who might have gone astray, but didn't. The bow is there. The rosin. He puts the rosin to the bow and sweeps the bow across it absentmindedly before the other fiddler asks him for a loan of it. Then hands are outstretched towards pints. They grasp them in a cheironomic sequence, and everyone imbibes in his or her own good time with inhaled breath, then an exhalation. Sleeves lift lazily in an off-beat chorus and wipe away the foamy white moustaches. It is nearly time to think of tunes, but not quite yet. Some of them are still in last night's time, when the owner of the bar forgot to call *time*.*

* All the italicised sections in this chapter are taken from *The New Grove Dictionary of Musical Instruments*, Macmillan, 1984.

Hurry the Jug

Time is never called in my recurring dream of pubs. The Belfast which these dreams inhabit is itself recurrent, changing, self-referential, in which the vestiges of antique maps become the map. I wander streets I try to rediscover in the waking world: dog-leg alleyways and laneways, early-electric down-town avenues, apparent cul-de-sacs which lead you through the colonnaded entrance to a shopping arcade. The pub might be located here, not in the arcade itself, but in some other gaslit annex of the cul-de-sac you hadn't noticed until then, until it strikes you that you've been here before, in this recurring or recurrent dream, a moment heralded by the melancholy repeated parp of a car-horn.

Because you think you know your way around, you end up sometimes getting lost – the city constantly evolves through synapses and mental lapses, forming bridges, short-cuts, contraflows and one-way systems. If the city is a piece of music, it depends on who's playing it, who's listening; and you are not the person you were a week ago, when last you visited the ornate Opera House. For one version of the pub is the Opera House in miniature, the doorposts to its booths surmounted by carved mythological beasts; a rampant elephant adorns the reredos. Three barmen flit like tenors in white aprons behind the long partitioned counter, their glossy Brylcreemed hair combed straight back on either side of their perfect centre partings. Silver sleeve-bands glint in the crooks of their snowy-white shirt-sleeves, and their movements have the practised negligence of men who've served their time, time and time again, responding gravely to the nods and winks of customers, anticipating every order. One hand is pulling pints while the other draws off half-uns from the optic. Brand-new packs of cigarettes appear by magic on the counter, divested of their cellophane and opened to reveal the contents like a pipe-organ.

Returning from the monumental urinals of porcelain and brass, you find the stained-glass door you came through leads now to a staircase. You find yourself in the upstairs lounge of somewhere else. It is a long thin room like an extended return, with wooden floor and ceiling and wooden church pews ranged along the two long walls, a wooden table in between. There's a tiny serving-hatch in one corner, and obviously I'm known here, since there is a pint of Guinness settling for me. And it would appear the night has not begun, since fiddle-cases and accordion-cases lie arranged, unopened on the benches. It's late and nearly empty. I realise now that this is where the sessions happen after hours. I know I am too early, but it doesn't matter; there's another drinker in the corner, and we'll find ways and means to pass the time.

Interlude

As I write, it is two minutes to midnight on the twelfth of December, 1994, and by the time I come to the end of this sentence – I am writing slowly, wondering what the next sentence might be – it will be the thirteenth. As it turns out, I have just watched one of those smart Guinness commercials in a break between the two halves of the American football big match (a game where time, as in this game, is often crucial, where the side trailing by five points at the end gets the ball back with 1.28 to play, and then it's all go, they must score a touch-down, but they don't – they ran out of time, or will run out of time). Anyway, the game is over, and I'm trying to describe this ad, which consists of this guy hunkered down and staring at – or rather, staring into – a freshly-poured pint. It's sifting and settling like a peaty burn tumbling into a blackbrown pool that momentarily reminds me of a line of Hopkins' prose about the incoming tide – 'then I saw it run browner, the foam dwindling and twitched into long chains of suds'. It takes me quite some time to find the reference, and I'm beguiled by other passages en route: his meditation on the word horn, *for example, or his entry for* Lent, *that time between times, where there will be 'No puddings on Sundays . . . meat only once a day . . . not to sit in an armchair except can work in no other way . . .'*

Back to Guinness: the camera, like the guy's eyes, zooms into the pint where the slowly-seething air-bubbles become microscoped and magnified, like deep-cleansing molecules with names like Surf and Dreft, penetrating and aerating the rope-coarse fibres of a silky-soft Angora sweater; but this is an illusion, since they now are Christmas baubles, or, more accurately, the music of the spheres, spinning orbs in Holst's Planet Suite, except that's not the music. The camera waltzes through a solar system till it centres on a planet and homes in.

The world dissolves into a Brueghel Tower of Babel, a Piranesi ziggurat with strange interior perspectives and misleading stairs. Now the camera's inside a room – a camera – inside the citadel, and it's packed with things, objets that might be trouvés, except it all happens so fast you don't get enough time to perceive them all, and you have to wait till the ad comes up again, and even then you don't quite get it. I end up recording it and rewinding it again and again. There's an old black Bakelite phone, a carved horse's head or giant chess-piece, a harp, a primitive Easter Island-type statuette, a wind-up set of joke false teeth, a vinyl record and a metronome, to name some; and there's a stop-watch. Some empty picture-frames. The TV you're watching is itself there. The pint itself is there, of course, settling on a leather-bound book. Then the camera zips out and rewinds through the other universe until it emerges in the 'real' world, where the pint has now settled, and it's time to lift it up and drink.

In some versions of the ad, the process is repeated twice. Or maybe the 'twice' version is the standard, and the 'single' is a deviation. It's a play on XX and X. Then the slogan, 'There's no Time like Guinness Time'. So, the inbuilt design flaw in Guinness – its reluctance to be poured and settle instantly in consumer-friendly fashion – is made into an ally. The act of waiting becomes an adventure; it is quality time, where the world is on pause, and you indulge in a kind of pipe dream. I have a vague recollection of a cigarette ad from the Sixties, where the slogan was 'Quality Time'. How times have changed! And does the settling time of the ad correspond to real time? I haven't measured them.

Certainly, the time is different from the old days. Then, Guinness stout, or 'Double X', as it was known, was poured, or rather, pulled differently: you pulled the handle of the pump away from you for 'high' (the white stuff) and pulled it back towards you for 'low' (the black stuff). The contemporary pump gives high and low in one go. Old barmen say the art of pouring a good pint disappeared with the onset of these single-action, one-gear pumps, the way they *say an automatic overrides the subtleties of clutch and stick control: you're not allowed to manage time. The sadly-defunct 'Single X', or porter, demanded a barman's highest skills: here, the high and low were in two separate barrels – hogsheads – with brass taps on them. You poured a bit of low, and then a bit of high, negotiating back and forth until you got the right proportions; then you skimmed the head with a spatula. You let it settle. Then you topped it up with another shot of high and let that settle. Finally, you skimmed the head again. It took practice. It took time.*

I now remember another conformation of this bar from the waking life of something like a quarter of a century ago: this was Pat's Bar, in Prince's Dock Street, now changed utterly, and modernised in *faux* Victoriana. My friends Mackers and Archie and I would find ourselves there after a circuitous pub-crawl that might include The Spanish Rooms, Kelly's Cellars, White's Tavern and The Ferryboat. Disembarking from The Ferryboat, we'd make our way through the docks, where sodium lights were mirrored in the slick black oily water and we breathed the turpentiney smell of pine planks stacked in warehouses. Freighters laden with grain and fruit creaked at their moorings, and sometimes the long blast of a fog-horn floated down the lough from far away, or the Pisan-leaning monumental Albert Clock would chime eleven. Arriving at Pat's, we would sidle in the side door and climb the rickety stairs to where we heard the bounce and swing of music. The pine floor would be heaving like a trampoline.

Then there are the pubs in country towns and villages where *fleadhanna* are held. I rarely dream about them, but from time to time they drift unsummoned into the inward eye. Typically, these pubs are long and narrow and telescopic, extending back from the front bar, to the back bar, to the kitchen with its cream-coloured Rayburn, to the annex, to the backyard with its open-air jacks. Beyond, there is an upward-sloping long straggly garden with spiky clumps of daffodils and rushes and a lean-to open shed against the high garden wall, where the proprietor has put out little wobbly tables and rickety chairs to take the *fleadh* overflow, and there's a plastic makeshift bar stocked with the basics – bottles of whiskey and vodka, bottles of stout and lager. There are candles stuck in bottles, swaying festively.

This is the sort of place where you might see three fiddle-players standing in a line in the cramped aisle between tables, all facing one way, belly to back, angled against the slope in some hieroglyphic mural statement, their bows and shadows flickering against the whitewashed wall like three thorn bushes bent by yesterday's prevailing wind: John Loughran, say, and Felix Kearney and Bobby Martin. And the usual percussion expert would have commandeered two empty Guinness bottles and be clicking them like Tío Pepe castanets, while his mate has taken up the ashtray tambourine.

The music is that great direct Tyrone rhythm full of draw and push, little leanings-into notes and off notes; no need to ornament except in tiny off-beat grace notes, the merest finger-flick. This music goes. It's like driving uphill, down-dale, riding with the peaks and troughs. Then you're bursting, swaying at the roofless jacks, pishing spattery patterns on the wall, and the old boy peeing next to you is saying, 'Powerful, powerful music, mighty', and both of you are gazing in your concentration at the stars. You hear the music back there float and lift beneath the corrugated-tin shed roof; the stars swirl by like dandelion seeds. Going back, you turn your head and in the dark beyond the candle-light, the daffodils have taken on a spiky yellow glow.

Then at rainy *fleadhanna* you'd find yourself in some rigged-up, jerry-built construction in the backyard, where the cute boy had put up a roof of heavy-duty polythene, this sheeting stretched between the yard wall and some teetering, precarious poles. From time to time the wobbly ceiling would yaw and sag beneath its weight of water, and the boy would come along as if he were a trident-bearer armed with brush, and spear it up against the plastic sheet to shuck the water off, and everyone would cheer as the edge of the crowd got soaked. Everyone is spluttering and laughing into their wet pints, and they don't give a damn, for this is any-weather music.

It's just as well, for any weather would occur, especially at those Easter *fleadhs* (a bastardised, if more common form of *fleadhanna*) I remember from the Sixties, held in border towns whose names all seemed to start with C: Carrickmacross, Cootehill, Castleblaney, Cavan, Clones. This is bumpy, mucky Patrick Kavanagh country, chock-a-block with drumlins, keshes, eskers, little scattered lakes and boggy hollows. Rain would pour down on the rushy thistly fields of smallholdings. Or sometimes it would snow, and I remember sleeping in a grain-loft on the verge of Clones, where a horizontal blizzard seethed through the gaps and chinks of the weatherbeaten pine planks. We lay there, Archie, Mackers and myself, our shoes full of animal feed or whatever it was, smoking cigarettes to give us the illusion of warmth. These were Carroll's, a mean cigarette that rasped your lungs, packed full with saltpetre to make them burn faster so you'd smoke more of them, and they'd spit and crackle halfway down, sending tiny sparks into the swirly dark. We would sleep in jaggy needly haystacks and stagger down a main street in the morning stuck with bits of straw. We slept in sheughs and ditches and the boots of cars, on benches in lounge bars and on the dance-floor of a derelict hotel.

We hitch-hiked. It was 1966, I think, and I was seventeen, when we decided to embark on our first *fleadh*. We knew by rumour or osmosis that the way you got there was to 'hitch-hike', but knew little of its methodology. We consulted veterans and old hands who would demonstrate the correct angle of the thumb and the cheerful, optimistic wave-on of the wrist and arm. It was important to be cheerful. Make eye-contact. Smile. Drivers were not charities: they would demand your company in exchange for transportation. I practised this in front of mirrors till my mother asked me what I was doing. When I told her that some of the lads were thinking of going to Castleblaney to hear some nice Irish music, she was aghast. She didn't know where Castleblaney was. Neither, come to think of it, did I. But she relented in the end and gave me a packed lunch, which I wrapped up in an ex-Army blanket for want of a sleeping bag, and I tied it all up with cord and slung it on my shoulder the way I thought you were supposed to, in that casual vagabondish way. My mother insisted I wear the top-coat she'd bought me in the Berlin Street pawn. She was right.

We split up into twos. Mackers went with someone else I can't remember. I went with Archie. Not knowing any better, we started off at Shaftesbury Square at the foot of the Lisburn Road, about half-a-mile out from Belfast city centre. Our elaborate gesticulations were met by uncomprehending stares. We stood and smiled and waved our thumbs at the traffic for about an hour, then decided to walk and wave our thumbs. I recall we walked as far as Hillsborough (some ten miles) before we thought we'd be better off splitting up: we remembered vaguely hearing that a boy and a girl were OK to hitch together, but two boys were bad news.

Having little conception of highways and byways, I found myself mostly on the byways, getting lifts for a mile or two, then walking. I was somewhere, where I'd never been before. The empty road wound upwards through the hills of South Armagh; I inhaled a cold clean wind. The sky was razor-blue. In the sporadic distance I would hear the faint hum of a motor-car, but then the wind would hush again, and it was gone into another distance.

Eventually, I got there. It was a one-street town I recollected having seen in photographs of Fair days. An old man leaned against the corner of the street, his greatcoat tied with yellow baling twine. He'd a fiddle in the crook of his arm and he was playing this wild strange tune. I stood on the edge of the town and gawped at him until he stopped.

'Excuse me, sir,' said I, 'am I in Castleblaney?' He peered at me from underneath his hat.

Naw,' said he, 'this is Castleblaney.'

The Dairy Maid

In the old times in Ireland, you know,
there were . . . what we call the Hiring Fairs.
That's where a boy or a girl would go
to the Hiring Fair
to hire out with a farmer as a farmer's servant,
or a dairy maid,
or a lad just as a farmer's servant round the yard,
helping him with his work on the land.

And this little girl
went to the Hiring Fair one day,
and what they used to do was stand in a line
all day. Nowadays,
they'd call it a queue.
But . . . oh, she stood all day
and every boy and girl in the whole line was taken
and she was left there alone
and nobody had taken her
and she was thinking of going home
and telling her parents that nobody had hired her . . .

And a funny little man came up to her
with a cocked hat on him.
Now, you wouldn't believe it, but this cocked hat
was coloured pink.
And he had a jacket with brass buttons on it,
and that was coloured a bright vivid
blue.
And he had a pair of knee britches on him

41

coloured emerald green.
And he had a pair of yellow stockings on him
up to the top of his knee britches,
and a pair of beautiful shiny brown boots on him,
and he had a big moustache
like the handle-bars of a bicycle
and a beard that was reaching down
to the brass buckle of his belt.

And he said, Did nobody take you, little girl?
Well, sir, she said, The way it is,
my parents told me to arrange
how much I'd be paid
for my service with you . . .
(because these were contracts for six months)
and, oh, he felt her biceps,
and he said, You're a strong little girl,
I'll pay you well.

Well, they travelled up a high hill
and down into a low valley
between green hedges and ditches,
and they left the hard road
and went on the soft road
between green hedges and ditches,
and they came then to a place
where there were trees growing both sides of the road –
what we'd call in literature, a sylvan tunnel –
and when they came out of the sylvan tunnel
the road took a sharp turn
to the left,
and they came into a clearing.

And there was the most comfortable
little thatched cottage
you ever saw.
What do you call that, little girl?, he said.
Oh, the hut, or the house, or whatever you please, sir.
No, no, he says, that's The Great Castle of Strawbungle.

He took a big iron key
out of his pocket
and he opened the door
and went in
and he threw a bottle of turf on the fire.
What do you call that, little girl?
That's the hot, or the heat,
or whatever you please, sir.
No, he said, that's Hot Cockelorum.

And the next thing, the cat came in
and stretched by the fire.
What do you call that, little girl?
That's the kit, or the cat, or whatever you please, sir.
No, no, he said, that's White-faced Simony.
And, she said, if I may make so bold, what
do I call you, sir?
Oh, my name's Dom Niperi Septoe, he said,
and I think we'll put down the kettle
and we'll make tay.

And you can picture her –
dutiful little girl that she was –
over to the crock of water with the pannikin,
filling the kettle.

What do you call that, little girl?
That's the wet, or the water, or whatever you please, sir.
No, he says, that's Pondelorum.
And she hung the kettle on the crane
over the fire,
and then he took off his boots –
he was tired after walking the whole day
through the fair –
What do you call those, little girl?
Well, your boots, your brogues,
whatever you please, sir . . .
No, he said, they're my Hay-down Treaders.

And then he rattled the knee of his knee-britches
at her,
And what do you call those, little girl?
Ah, your britches, your breeks, whatever you please, sir.
No, he said, they're my Fortune's Crackers.
And he said, now,
while we're waiting for the kettle to boil,
I'll show you upstairs
to where you're going to sleep.
I'll show you to your room
where you're going to live
for the next six months.

And going up the stairs, he says,
What do you call those, little girl?
Oh, the steps, or the stairs, or whatever you please, sir.
No, he said, that's The Wooden Hill.
And he threw open a door at the top of the stairs
and he showed her her bed in her room.
What do you call that, little girl?
Oh, the bunk, or the bed, or whatever you please, sir.
No, he said, that's the Barnacle.

And they had supper
and they milked the cow
and they locked up
and away to bed for the night.

And in the middle of the night
there was a rap, rap – a knock at his door.
What's wrong, little girl? he said.

Rise up from your Barnacle, Dom Niperi Septoe,
and put on your Fortune's Crackers
and your Hay-down Treaders
and come down The Wooden Hill
because White-faced Simony
has a spot of Hot Cockelorum on his tail
and if we don't pour Pondelorum on it quick
The Great Castle of Strawbungle
will be in Hot Cockelorum.

Now, I knew that little girl years later,
said Séamus Ennis,
and whenever we'd be playing music
we'd have to be careful
not to play 'The Smoky House'.
Because if we did, she'd run a mile.
So we never played it
after we found out that she was allergic
to this reel.

He took up a whistle and he played a reel he called 'The Smoky House', or, 'Whatever you Please'.

The Happy Days of Youth

The first school essay I remember writing was called 'How to Light a Fire'. It was in the days when all of Belfast burned coal and the factories were like convoys of destroyers, their tall smoke-stacks belching out in chorus as they wove their fat skeins of smog across the city . . .

It is freezing cold: one of those February days when, perversely, the marble-shooting season would begin and your knuckles are skinned and raw, chapped blue and purple from squinting and shooting 'marlies' in their complicated planetary rituals and ricocheting paths. Or two of us are sent out into an opalescent fog to skid and skate across the black bottle-glass rink of the granite yard. We are the milk-collectors. The galvanised-iron milk-crate burns frostily into our palms and fingers. It clinks and tingles as we teeter back, the pair of us, like out-of-synch zinc buckets on a milkmaid's swaying yoke.

I step into the sudden fug of the classroom radiator-warmth. When we take the bottles out they're frozen solid half-way down their half-pint length. We rack and clunk them up like snowman soldiers on the regimental cast-iron pipes. Gradually, a sour-sweet thaw will blend its milk-aroma with the other fug ingredients: chalk-dust, pencil-shavings, plasticine, sweaty socks, damp raincoats, schoolbag leather, ink, lino, blotting-paper, oak and varnish, the interiors of pencil-boxes, the exhalation of our breath against the de La Salle Brother's blackboard-black soutane. Snow, too, is in the air; it will soon snow down like algebra. After the preliminary joy of crowding to the window, we settle down to write: 'First, you take a bundle of sticks . . .' No, 'First you get your coal. You go out to the coal-shed.'

It was a bunker, really, brick-built against the yard wall, open to the freezing air, since no one thought of a lid. In snowy weather, black lumps sparkled craggily below the snow-cap. The shovel grated wetly as it scraped into the aperture. The coal clunked into the scuttle with a bumpy, hollow sound: a tiny, momentary, melismatic avalanche, each daily rhythm different to the next, but in its special chunkiness of timbre, reminding you of yesterday. You tilted your shoulder and your arm ached at the elbow as you took the strain. Underfoot was slush. You picked and slipped your way across it to the kitchen door and worked the tick-tock of the latch.

Kneeling before the still-warm empty grate, you tore and crumpled up the *Irish News*. Or, the *Irish News and Belfast Morning News*, as it was more grandiosely known then. The sticks, bundled up in hairy coarse string, were purchased from a ragged man who wheeled his wares in a pram and called them out at intervals along the early-darkening street, until the gas-lamps came on one by one. Then he was gone into the fog. I felt he was a sleeping-partner of the coal-brick man, whose flat hand-cart bore a ziggurat of steaming coal-brick still hot from the press. His shouts of 'c-o-o-a-a-al b-r-r-e-e-e-k' lingered in the air long after he had passed.

Burning coal-brick is a way of passing time. It is a unit of time. You know how many bricks will last a week; you know the time to put the coal-brick on, when the coal has settled to a deep glow. I remember listening to its algorithmic spits and hisses on a gloomy Sunday, curled up in a fireside chair. My father, in an absentminded ritual, has picked up the melodeon. The yellowed bone buttons tick and click through the smog of the room as his fingers wander through a tune, 'The Rose of Arranmore', then, 'Nearer My God to Thee', perhaps; it's Sunday, after all. He wheezes sympathetically as the bellows wheeze and the bass reiterates its off-beat counterpoint, the spoon-keys struck apparently at random. Years later, I will learn to play it, or at least be able, as they say, to knock a few tunes out of it. In the meantime, 'How to Light a Fire'? I've forgotten what it was I wrote then, whatever verbal contours I described. But I vaguely recall its formal, simple elegance and its logical progression down the page – a way of writing far removed from the baroque adventures detailed in the many rubric pockets and the holes in pockets in such essays as 'The Autobiography of a Penny', or (I'm making this one up) 'The Story of a Flute'.

Hard to Fill

I hesitate to say '*my* flute'. Some musicians are superstitious about their instruments, and prefer to think of themselves as custodians rather than owners: the instrument, after all, has usually been around a lot longer than they have, and will likely be around for a lot longer; it has been through several or many hands, and if it could speak, might cast aspersions on its present companion's musical abilities. Use of the Irish language, with its hazy concept of ownership, might be pertinent here: 'my flute' would be *an fliúit s'agamsa*, or 'the flute which is *at* me'.

At any rate, the barrel-joint of this flute before me is stamped:

D'ALMAINE & CO

LATE

GOULDING & D'ALMAINE

SOHO SQUARE

LONDON

which, according to Lyndesay G. Langwill's *An Index of Musical Wind Instrument Makers*, dates it between 1836–58, and it probably belongs to the earlier part of that period, given the advertisement that Goulding is no longer with D'Almaine. The flute also has a little corroborating catch to it: Sam Murray, the flute-maker who sold me this instrument (or rather, it was partner to an elaborate swap) tells me that it's not a D'Almaine at all. He picks up the foot-joint and prises out the little brass pins which hold the C# key in place; he turns it over, and there, under the touch of the key, are the initials 'A.L.', the hidden maker's mark of Alexander Liddle who spent some time with D'Almaine and later set up shop on his own at 24 Chenies Street (1847–54) and then at 35 Devonshire Street (1854–73).

This is a six-keyed flute of Jamaican cocus-wood, weathered to a rich dark chocolate brown with oxblood striations glinting under the immediate surface. It's an early Victorian machine, but it still retains many of the characteristics of its direct precursor, the baroque one-keyed flute (essentially, a wooden tube with six finger-holes and an embouchure, or mouth-hole). Theoretically, the single key made the baroque flute into a fully chromatic instrument; in practice, many cross-fingered notes were deficient in intonation, but some consider this weakness to be a strength because the player is forced to humour and to shade notes, so that each note has its own distinctive timbre. Nevertheless, these inherent characteristics led makers to add progressively more keys in order to simplify chromatic intonation; so this Liddle is a product of that development. Like the baroque flute, it sounds best in the keys of D and G, and this makes it ideal for Irish traditional music.

Classical musicians, however, became increasingly dissatisfied with this 'simple-system' flute. The urge for complete evenness of tone over the chromatic range, allied to the expansion and increasing regimentation of the orchestra and the building of bigger concert halls to accommodate the bourgeoisie, led eventually to its demise. It was gradually replaced by the radical new design of Theobald Boehm, who in 1847 devised an instrument with a cylindrical bore (as opposed to the conical bore of the old flute) and enormous tone-holes which could not be covered by the fingers, but demanded an intricate system of pads, levers and springs to enable each key to open independently as well as interact with the others. The result, in the opinion of many, is a different instrument entirely; and certainly, it is disparaged by many traditional players as a class of typewriter. Whatever the merits of the case, the so-called 'simple-system' flute became obsolete for orchestral purposes and passed into the hedge-school underworld of Irish music.

Traditional music has probably more practitioners now than at any time in its history, and the demand for simple-system flutes is such that it cannot be satisfied by antique instruments; so new flute-makers like Sam Murray have begun to take the old design on board and modify it.

We are in Sam's workshop at 1 Exchange Place, Belfast. Exchange Place is, in Belfast parlance, an 'entry': a narrow lane between two streets; a backwater or a short-cut, a deviation from the beaten path.

Exchange Place *is* an entry: we talk and breathe in an exhalation, a many-layered scent of shellac, beeswax, raw and boiled linseed oil, tallow, almond oil, aromatic blackwood shavings, nitric acid and ammonia. I believe you can smell the blue steel blades and boxwood handles of the antique tools: gravers, gouges, chisels, pliers, diamond files and flat files, pincers, chasers. You pick one up and feel its oily-sharp edge with grainy specks of sawdust on it. Then there are the immense solid lathes with their treadleboards and black cast-iron flywheels and counterweights, their headstocks and their tailstocks, their spindles and their mandrels. One of the lathes is made by Kennan of Fishamble Street in Dublin, whose premises were Neale's Music Hall where Handel premièred his *Messiah*. This Kennan lathe passed into the custodianship of The Irish Horological Society and resides here now because Sam believes that instruments and tools are not mere servants, but collaborators in our fate. The other lathe, made in 1806 by the sonorous firm of Holtzapffel & Deyerlein, has some other complicated history attached to it. The pair of them have weight, a gloomy pondering solidity that reassures you by its presence and its earned place here. These are lathes which were broken up and which languished in sheds and backyards till some curious, wheeling-dealing, slow catenation of events led to their resurrection and their redeployment.

And this is not to speak of the unspeakable archaeological layers of things strewn and assembled on every available surface in the workshop: pins, papers, screws, tobacco tins and coffee jars, thread, waxed paper, empty bobbins, walrus tusk, billiard balls, sealing-wax and string, envelopes, cigar-boxes, empty glasses, tannin-encrusted teacups, bus tickets, knives, a bottle of Angostura bitters, a drawing-plate, a bicycle repair-kit, two old trade tin trays (Ross's Mineral Waters and Buckfast Tonic Wine) with rusted pocks in them, bills, invoices, a blue tin of Vaseline, Christmas cards and postcards, a blowtorch, fluxes, solders, coils of silver wire, brass tubing, wine-corks, an old cardboard advertisement for Bassett's Liquorice Allsorts, brass plate, a Swiss Army knife, dust, unaccountable detritus and filings of long-gone operations, a Bo-Peep matchbox which rattles with brass thumb-tacks when you pick it up, washers, drill-bits, oil-cans, tea-pots, files, gimlets, scissors, a copy of the *Irish News* from last year, a shrivelled chip, Kirby grips, bulldog clips, Jubilee clips and paper clips, a square damp packet of Saxa salt, Blu-Tack, bits of putty, sealing-wax, a little paper packet of cigarette-lighter flints, a candle-stub, a Zippo lighter, cotton-wool, a sticky tin of Tate & Lyle's Golden Syrup, wisps of steel wool, and the blue glint of methylated spirits shivering in a glass square-shouldered glass-stoppered bottle against a stained, scarred patch of the workbench; on a window-sill, three little tinker-made tin inkwell-shaped receptacles with milled brass screwtops, containing pumice, tripoli and rouge, each bearing the original early Victorian price of three shillings (3/-).

Besides all this, of course, are various flutes in various stages of manufacture, repair or disrepair. They remind me of other flutes that have passed through my hands. The first was exhumed from the attic dark of a friend's house and given to me, as someone who might be able to 'do something with it'. I have it still: as you undo the hooks and eyes of its box and flip open the lid, it's like breathing in the woody incense of a pencil-box. The flute itself is made in boxwood by an obscure early nineteenth-century Dublin maker called Garret. Its sound is delicate yet firm, with a surprisingly strong bottom D (a crucial note on the flute), but it never could compete in Irish traditional music sessions, at least not in those held in pubs. It's pitched a little lower than modern concert pitch and it's difficult to get in tune with modern fixed-pitch instruments – you have to overblow it, and it doesn't function quite right when you do. But it's good for kitchen music, and kitchen music can be the best, with two or three musicians and some friends.

Having been given the flute, I felt obliged to try and learn it. The fingering, it seemed, was much like that of the tin whistle: all you had to do was to learn how to blow. So I would lie on the floor and stare at the ceiling and blow till my eyes popped out because other flute-players – real flute-players, that is – told me that was how they learned. The theory was, it developed your diaphragm muscles, but since you used to blow until you got dizzy, it was probably just as well you were lying down. Or you would stand up in the bathroom because its tiles and mirrors amplified whatever little noise you made, and you looked into a mirror as you learned to play, to check the fixed smile of your embouchure and the way your fingers moved. It's a version of what Charlie Parker called 'woodshedding' when he was seriously learning the sax or the ax or the horn, or whatever they tagged it, the way marijuana was 'mezzirolls' or 'sticks', and jobs were 'gigs'. You went out to the woodshed where you could be alone and wouldn't freak your folks, and you made all the mistakes you needed, because that's how you would learn. So the bathroom became *my* woodshed.

I started gradually to learn that a flute is not a tin whistle. Though the fingering for both is more or less identical, you can't hit the notes the same way because of the cramped posture of your hands, the added stretch, the very thickness of the flute with its sometimes painful pressure against the inside of the palm-knuckle of the left forefinger. Then there is the question of the breath and how you take it, and how to let it out. The flute resists your breath in a necessary way; the whistle offers no resistance, and the breathing is very different.

But gradually, you start to get a buzz. You learn to 'fill' the flute. You feel the flute vibrate when it is warm, and the little coin-columns of air stacked beneath your fingertips dance up and down like mercury thermometers, all registering different bouncy volatiles of temperature. The sound begins to carry, to lift, and it's surprising how a flute carries: when you leave the session for the bog or loo or bathroom, it's the voice you hear above the box and pipes and fiddles and guitars. From out there, all the different sonic components get blurred and scrambled into different frequencies and sometimes other music leaks and filters through into it from another session in the pub next door. It reminds me of the noise of an old Clydesdale Bakelite radio, as I spun its thick, half-crown-sized knob across the lighted blips of stations called Athlone, Vienna, Hilversum, Helsinki. Symphonies were passed by in an instant as you plunged into a storm of Morse and bleeping static; Arabs playing clarinets would flit by through Saharas of black noise and muezzins could be heard across the city till they dwindled underneath a sudden blast of rock. Then you went back to the session.

The flute is handy for a session. Broken into three or four pieces, it is easily concealed; and it is useful, sometimes, to adopt the posture of a non-musician. It is often wrapped in newspaper – the *Connacht Tribune* springs to mind – and slid into the inside pocket of a shiny blue serge jacket. Then, produced unostentatiously, it might add a new dimension to whatever's going on and sometimes, when the fiddle-players stop, their 'breather' will be this smoker of a fluter who's been doing sixty most of his life, but plays as if he's got Aeolus and several bags of wind beneath his belt.

I think of Pakie Duignan, for example, who was truly great and

liked nothing better than a pint and a cigarette and some tunes in
the offing. He had the hands of one who had worked long years in
the Arigna coal-mines and I recall how he would sometimes prop
a Sweet Afton between his thick fingers while he played. His way
of breathing was a joy: it had economy and grace and power; his
management of time was perfect. He had the time to hit whatever
note it was that came next, then to extend the breath into the next
phrase like a sudden almost-visible extension of the room, as if this
phrase had yearned to be united with its predecessor, and now they
were together. Then he'd cut the end of that phrase and wander
off into the split chink of a twilight zone, momentarily. Normal
business would resume some time, but in this instant he had gone
down steps he'd never seen till then, that led down to a dark harbour
where water clucked against the boats and rocks and a constellation
could be seen reflected.

Then you were off in a strange hooker out of Carna, bound for
Inishbofin, as red sails set in the sunset. Salt crystals sparkled on
the dark planks. It was a wedding eve. When you got there, you
dropped into The Harbour Bar, and there was Pakie at the far end
of the bar. In mid-phrase, and without missing a beat, he raised his
right hand from a G-note in a salutation, since the G ended at his
left hand and the right hand was defunct for that split second in
its nicotined arrest.

So, I remember fiddle-players with cigarettes poised between two
fingers of their bow-hand, and the ash would wave and sprinkle in
a silent musicology across their trouser-knees; or the cigarette that
drooped between a player's lips would let drop a little grub of ash
into an *f*-hole of the fiddle, where it disintegrated as it crashed into
the ersatz 'Stradivari' label. Then knees were dusted off, someone
rosined up, and a fitful shaft of sunlight would illuminate the
dust-motes like a dissolute snowstorm souvenir.

I would watch the players split the cellophane on flat cigarette
packs with their yellowed thumb-nails, then zip it off and squash it
and throw it to the floor, where it would uncrumple silently. They
pushed the packet open from the bottom with their thumbs. They
slipped off the silver foil and crushed it, then rolled it into a ball and
flicked it towards a corner. Then two or three, whatever cigarettes
would be extruded, proffered ceremoniously to all in turn. Someone

else would have this brand-new Zippo lighter which he *had* to try out – it would appear already lit by casual magic. It would be handed round and admired for the lifetime guarantee of its thick burnished steel casing and the satisfactory rasp of the milled edge of the wheel against the flint, against your thumbprint.

Everyone inhaled in different tempos, like a quartet score with puffs of smoke for notes unfurled in wispy accidentals. Then four half-smoked cigarettes would smoulder untouched in a big round tin Bass ashtray with its silent red triangle, until someone, in a fit of inhaled solitude, recalled whatever tune it was he meant to go into the last time round, before they'd stopped to smoke. He would play a bar or two and everyone would join in. Then by the end of *that* set, they would reach for the remnant cigarettes to find they'd dwindled into extinct butts attached to worms of ash. So, cigarettes and music are also a measurement of time.

It was about this time I bought an old Hawkes Siccama system flute for sixty pounds. This system, patented by the London maker Abel Siccama, was basically a 'simple-system', with some Boehm-like 'improvements': the E and A holes were dramatically enlarged and moved to 'musically-correct' positions, out of reach of the relevant fingers, so keys had to be added to accommodate these holes. I was very impressed by this flute at the time, because compared to the genteel quiet Garret, the Hawkes sounded like a trumpet. But there were drawbacks, as in any system, some of which I didn't recognise at the time. Its loudness drew attention to the technical uncertainties of a novice, who, in his eagerness to be heard, blows too hard and thus goes sharp. The novelty E and A keys worked OK if you were playing a full note with them, but their action didn't respond fast enough to rolls.

To define a roll is difficult – it must be heard in order to be understood, or grasped. Basically, a roll consists of a five-step rhythmical cluster: you play the note to be rolled, then a note above the anchor note (the 'cut'), then the note, then a note below the note (the 'tip'), and finally the note again. How you play the cut and the tip depends on whatever instrument you're playing, and how you want to emphasise or shape the roll; they consist of the merest flick of the fingers, and seem to exist outside conventional time, since the quintuple movement happens in triplet time.

Once you learn how to do it, it is tempting to roll all over the place and reduce the structure of the tune to a tasteless slabber of ornament. It is doubly tempting because its arabesque fits nicely into the received mythology of Irish music as a *Book of Kells* cottage industry with anonymous scribes passing time or doing time in endless loops and spirals. So, the fiddle-player Michael Coleman has been deified because he rolled a lot. Some think he rolled too much, and might prefer the playing of his contemporary Paddy Killoran, who got great bounce and rasp from the bow and used the roll for occasional rhythmic variation. Sometimes it seemed as if the time of the tune had been momentarily changed, and you glimpsed another time, another destination, beyond the current run of notes; as if the bus company had found room for one more intermediary stop, yet still managed to de-bus its final passengers on schedule. At the terminus, in his dimly-lit cab, the driver would reach up and actively wind back the destinations with the little cast aluminium movie-camera handle in the ceiling. He would watch the names reel backwards through his periscope. Did he read them mirror-fashion, like a printer, or did the periscope contain an extra mirror? Or, had he memorised the number of twists?

By now, I imagine Killoran and the band have just finished one of those big New York ex-pat *ceilis*. They are sitting on the stage still, their instruments not yet put to bed. They are leaning forward towards each other, talking, smoking, drinking beer from long-necked bottles. The dancers have gone. The hall is lighted by dim oyster-shell wall-lights and two red neon EXIT signs. The dance floor is littered with crushed, danced-on cigarette ends. Two boys are cleaning up. They have hooked the chairs upside down in fours on top of the little round tables placed against the walls. They sweep their wide soft brushes in broad loops and spirals across the strewn floor as if wiping clean the ghost impressions of a thousand interlocking dance-step diagrams; occasionally they meet up in a grave, apparently unpractised gesture, then push off like a pair of skaters who will end their programme with an ornate reconciliation. Up on the band-stand the second fiddle-player is asking Killoran what it was he did with the second part of the turn the third time round in 'The Humours of Whiskey'. 'Well,' says Killoran, 'you kind of double up the time.' He leans down and picks up the fiddle which has been placed on its edge by his chair with the bow resting delicately along the side. 'Something like this . . .'

I am trying to remember what it might be myself, and, sitting at the table, I switch off the portable Corona and pick up the Alexander Liddle D'Almaine and run my hands across the first few notes.

The Steampacket

Now I can visualise Seamus Tansey's fingers undulating up and down the scale in that preliminary twiddle musicians fall into before the tune or in a lull between tunes: not so much a warming up as an exploration, seeking reassurance that the notes you might require are there beneath your hands' experimenting. The fingers fall into a matrix of the weight and depth of notes and suddenly a tune suggests itself.

He starts off with 'The Lady on the Island', and I'm reminded once again how this reel reminds me of 'The Sailor on the Rock' in its melodic structure and nomenclature. He plays it five times, developing a theme that splits into two themes about the third time round: rolling it one way this time and another the next, at the same time toying with that Tansey stock-in-trade, blowing the high notes low and vice versa, jumping octaves all the time. He does a final ornamental flourish and runs into 'The Little Pack of Tailors'. It's a great change, and one I'd never contemplated until then. For a start, 'The Lady' is very rarely used as a first tune, because it's so handy for going into from another tune, or for tacking on to the end of a set if you can think of nothing else. It's a kind of floating tune which gets promiscuously attached to other tunes; come to think of it, it's a variant of 'Rolling in the Rye-grass'.

Conversely, 'The Little Pack' is a good first tune because it's steady and has big long notes in it you can hang on to, and then you can accelerate it bit by bit till you're at ease with speed, and the second tune will probably start on a jump and then you really hit the beat. Tansey hits 'The Little Pack of Tailors' like a steampacket at full blast in mid-Atlantic, and leaves 'The Lady on the Island' an already far-away iota on the dark horizon. He plays it five times too and then he changes into what? – 'The Sailor on the Rock', and I'm terribly pleased because I'd half-anticipated it. The set takes on a beautiful poetic justice, with its notions of abandonment and business, its rhyming of the lonely sailor with this mischievous faction of a medieval guild; as if the tags and labels, tired of being elastically attached to whatever garments were on purchase in the shop that day, had floated off at midnight, and now were flittering in convoy through the half-lit fragrances department, admiring names like Guerlain, Kathleen Mary Quinlan, and doing loop-the-loops round L'Air du Temps. For though the name is not the thing itself and though the name is not the tune, it can suggest a reciprocity of feeling; it can summon up relations that were dormant but perhaps intended, preconceived or preordained by other players long before our time. Such is Tansey's logic.

I burst into applause, and realise I'm listening to a tape I made the year I bought the Sony portable: now I hear the ghostly presence of my own applause back there, back then, I come back with a jolt to *now*. My eyes come to. I'm sitting in the kitchen, feeling dislocated. I'd been on a trip. It was back in 1978 and we were in the Hotel Carlton, Belleek, County Fermanagh, just across the road from the famous Pottery. I no longer have the Sony – I gave it to the flute-player Desi Wilkinson – but I can visualise it sitting on the floor beneath a table in the Carlton. It's nearly the size of a bag of sugar and about twice as heavy, with its matt black steel casing and its grainy black leather holder, its chunky buttons. I recall their click, their springy pressure on my fingertips.

The tape runs on. Now there's gabble round the table. Because the music is so good and the Sony was the last thing on my mind, I'd left it running absentmindedly. I identify the voices: Gary Hastings, Gerry O'Donnell, Maura McConnell, Deirdre Shannon, me. Others. Random conversation, laughter, fore-and-background clinking noises. Then Tansey does his preliminary twiddle again and a hush descends on the murky lounge bar. He soars into 'The Battering Ram' – not the standard version, but the one he got from Jim Donoghue, the great Sligo tin-whistle-player who perversely played a 'C' whistle ('D' is standard) out of the side of his mouth, and produced a great strong flute-like tone full of wood and embouchure and breath, jumping octaves; and he put a funny twist into this jig, reversing it and generally standing phrases on their heads. Tansey imputes many of his stylistic traits to Donoghue, and this tune is a tribute, an *hommage*, a dedication, Tansey playing it as beautifully as he can because he loves the playing of Jim Donoghue, and he is beholden to him.

But Tansey is his own man too, and knows he's good. All great musicians recognise their ancestry and pay respect to it, and they know the thing is bigger than the sum of individuals: it progresses in a multiplicity of exponential steps and fractal variations; and stepping on a butterfly way back there in the past will have an unforeseen chaotic implication for the present or the future. Because a note was bent back then, the whole tune has taken on another bent or warp or woof, and sometimes, someone will put in another bend that gets back to the source, just as the flooded Mississippi breaks its banks and takes a straighter, faster course between its hitherto meanderings. The river-bend becomes an ox-bow lake. Whole towns are abandoned.

It's all in flux. In bars in towns called Memphis, Thebes and Cairo, the river-pilots gather to discuss their current Nile, or what *was* current yesterday, and prognosticate its future course, the shifting of its underwater reefs and bars and snags. To be a river-pilot you must have a photographic memory, or rather a filmic memory, since the images are never static: soundings must be taken all the time. The pilot scans the water constantly, reading it for change, for dissolution and establishment of hazards. He manipulates the big clock-shaped wheel with handles calibrated at five-minute intervals, negotiating time and tide, while his leadsmen chant out the soundings: 'M-a-r-k three! . . . M-a-r-k three! . . . Quarter-less-three! . . . Half twain! . . . M-a-r-k twain! . . .'

Musicians, borne on a spate of music, take their soundings; hearing something new, they search the memory-bank for parallels and precedents, getting its approximation, its relative shape. A rough internal course is plotted out before embarking; fingers mime the notes. Then the details – little snags and twists – are filled in, or attempted. Some people are better at this than others, and some tunes are easier to 'lift' than others; some put up resistance. Sometimes the best way to learn these is by leaving them to one side for a day or two and not think about them, till they come as if by chance from some obscure source in the brain: the fingers find the pattern without conscious effort. But of course the instinct is instructed by years of listening. We drift on in the wide, swift current of the music, trusting to our memories and to past associations.

Mark Twain wrote:

And how easily and comfortably the pilot's memory does its work; how placidly effortless is its way; how *unconsciously* it lays up its vast stores, hour by hour, day by day, and never loses or mislays a single valuable package of them all! Take an instance. Let a leadsman cry, 'Half twain! half twain! half twain! half twain! half twain!' until it becomes as monotonous as the ticking of a clock; let conversation be going on all the time, and the pilot be doing his share of the talking, and no longer consciously listening to the leadsman; and in the midst of this endless string of half twains let a single 'quarter twain!' be interjected, without emphasis, and then the half twain cry go on again, just as before: two or three weeks later that pilot can describe with precision the boat's position in the river when that quarter twain was uttered, and give you such a lot of head-marks, stern-marks, and side-marks to guide you, that you ought to be able to take the boat there and put her in that same spot again yourself! The cry of 'quarter twain' did not really take his mind from his talk, but his trained faculties instantly photographed the bearings, noted the change of depth, and laid up the important details for future reference without requiring any assistance from *him* in the matter. If you were walking and talking with a friend, and another friend at your side kept up a monotonous repetition of the vowel sound A, for a couple of blocks, and then in the midst interjected an R, thus, A, A, A, A, A, R, A, A, A, etc., and gave the R no emphasis, you would not be able to state, two or three weeks afterward, that the R had been put in, nor be able to tell what objects you were passing at the moment it was done. But you could if your memory had been patiently and laboriously trained to do that sort of thing mechanically.

from *Life on the Mississippi*

Of course, a prodigious memory is no guard against the unexpected. A big rise in the river would bring down a swarm of timber-rafts, coal barges and trading scows. The law required such craft to keep a light burning; and the law was often broken. The boys in such a scow are down below, carousing, and the pilot's nudging his steamboat up an island 'chute' as dark as the inside of a cow. But the sound of fiddling is heard just soon enough to veer off. The revellers bring up their lantern then, and curse the pilot till the air turns blue. Then they drift by in the ever-lengthening dark, and go back to drinking whiskey.

The Humours of Whiskey

*Whisky (Ir. and U.S. **whiskey**) (h)wis'ki, n. as legally defined, a spirit obtained by distillation from a mash of cereal grains saccharified by the diastase of malt: formerly applicable to a spirit obtained from potatoes, beetroot, or any starch-yielding material: a glass of such spirits.*

Chambers 20th Century Dictionary (1983 edition)

'Whiskey', of course, is from Irish or Scots Gaelic *uisce*, 'water', as in 'vodka'.

> If water was whiskey and I was a duck
> I'd jump to the bottom and never come up . . .

Whiskey is *poitín*, or vice versa, since *poitín* is, according to Dinneen, 'whiskey made in private stills', a fine distinction to *Chambers'* censorious 'Poteen, Irish whiskey illicitly distilled'. (But then *Chambers* is a Scottish, or Scotch dictionary.) *Poitín* is 'little pot', or 'little still', and poteen is known as 'still', especially in the North of Ireland. And in Northern jargon, 'Parliament whiskey' is what you buy in the spirit grocer's or wherever; so, plain 'whiskey' is sometimes poteen. Poteen is mountain dew, not the fizzy Mountain Dew in cans, which I first encountered in the USA and was most disappointed by. And in the USA – or in North Carolina at least – the fiddler and moonshine-maker Tommy Jarrell sings the song quoted above and usually calls his product 'brandy'. Elsewhere, it's 'white lightnin''. In Western parts of Ireland they are fond of a drop of the *cratur*:

Here's to the cratur, the best thing in nature
For drowning your sorrows and raising your joys . . .

Mící Mac Gabhann, whose *Rotha Mór an tSaoil* (The Great
Wheel of Life) is an iconic account of the Irish labourer abroad,
relates how children were fed poteen on a daily basis to ward off
the whooping-cough and diarrhoea, much as laudanum was dosed
out in the nineteenth century. Tom Lenihan from Miltown Malbay,
who sang the above song, remembers much the same. Tom wore
the Pioneer pin signifying total abstinence, for drinking poteen was
a 'reserved' sin. In those days, poteen tended to be made from
malted barley, so perhaps there was some goodness in it. These
days, it is more likely to be made from sugar, so it's really a kind
of white rum.

Still, there are regional variations in poteen, as there are in music,
and music seems to be affected by the stuff, and vice versa, since
the spire of St Malachy's Church in Belfast was 'removed, with
advantage, for the tolling of the great bell in it interfered with
the satisfactory maturing of the whiskey in Messrs. Dunville's
adjacent distillery'. This long-gone-out-of-business Dunville's is a
funny whiskey. I once procured an ancient bottle of it, labelled
'Dunville's Special Liqueur Whisky' – without the Irish 'e'. But
then, Dunville's was a Northern whiskey, and I remember the
bottle of curiously-labelled 'Irish Scotch' on the special shelf of the
Harbour Bar. Some form of politics was at work, or economics.
The Dunville's Whisky, by the way, was brilliant: mellow, smoky,
smooth, powerful, deep beneath its sniffed aroma, redolent with
time and satisfactory maturing. This was a whiskey you drank neat,
or with a hint of water to bring out the flavour, and I could never
understand how rock stars, for example, would drink whiskey and
Coke; perhaps their appetites had been depraved by electricity. But
then tastes differ, *chacun à son goût*, one man's meat . . .

When you buy land, you buy stones
When you buy meat, you buy bones

Such was the philosophy of the butcher in Miltown Malbay,
whose window-display consisted of a steel rail with a pig's trotter
hung at one end and an oxtail at the other. And it was down around
these parts I first encountered 'punch' – not the usual hot toddy of

whiskey, hot water, lemon and cloves, nor the awful concoction of wine and citrus juice and sugar made up specially for office parties – no, this punch was poteen and hot water and *butter*, reminding one that the tea-and-yak-butter of Tibet might not be so unlikely after all. For, putting aside our momentary prejudice of taste, suspending disbelief, we took one cautious sip and then a bigger one. Two pint glasses later – clock time, here, is not a consideration – we were literally singing its praises:

> If I were sick and very bad
> And was not able to go or stand
> I would not think it at all amiss
> To pledge my shoes for a jug of punch . . .

So, poteen has its different twangs and accents, different tangs on the tongue and palate. I have sampled various fruit poteens, in which the perpetrator has marinated oranges or whatever in it; and it is not unusual for poteen to be dyed with tea and put into Bushmills bottles or even Lucozade bottles to look like beverages approved by Parliament.

Like any illicit drug, poteen carries a big freight of mythology. 'Take a drink of water in the morning, and you're drunk again.' 'Sure I drunk a bottle of it and in the morning, sure my head was clear as a bell.' 'Drink that stuff and you'll go blind.' There are songs and yarns and poems about specific gravities of poteen-making. Gaugers are evaded. Boasts and toasts are made. The dead come to life. Many truths are told. For John Millington Synge on Aran, it is the spirit of a people:

> The rain continues; but this evening a number of young men were in the kitchen mending nets, and the bottle of poteen was drawn from its hiding-place.
>
> One cannot think of these people drinking wine on the summit of this crumbling precipice; but their grey poteen, which seems to bring a shock of joy to the blood, seems predestined to keep sanity in men who live forgotten in these worlds of mist.
>
> I sat in the kitchen part of the evening to feel the gaiety that was rising, and when I came into my own room after dark, one of the sons came in every time the bottle made its round, to pour me my share.
>
> J.M. Synge, *The Aran Islands*

This is a strange poteen-induced passage in which time and space and custom have undergone some tremors of dimension, and come out slightly wrong. Synge has staggered off to bed. The young fishermen are perplexed. They seemed to be getting on so well with him. The foreigner had just played a rather stiffly-classical version of 'The Black Rogue' on his violin or fiddle. It didn't really swing, but, sure, the man was doing his best and didn't Tom Pheait's Nóra Bhuí get up and dance to it, and then Synge takes another swig and he's telling them about the boulevards of Paris and the great world that's in it. He had introduced a new technology:

> One evening I found her trying to light a fire in the little side-room of her cottage, where there is an ordinary fireplace. I went in to help her and showed her how to hold up a paper before the mouth of the chimney to make a draught, a method she had never seen. Then I told her of men who live alone in Paris and make their own fires that they may have no one to bother them.

This, too, was the poteen talking. And right enough, he seemed to go all gloomy for a minute, but the next thing, he was doing magic tricks with bits of string and entertaining the assembled company. And then he staggers off to bed. The young fishermen have heard of English reserve. Perhaps this is an English custom. Perhaps there comes a stage when Englishmen can only drink alone. And the circle of the clockwise poteen bottle cannot be unbroken. Etiquette demands it. Reiteration cannot skip a beat. It would be like cutting out a triplet in the tune. So they drink their grey poteen well into the blue-grey limestone dawn, reminding me that poteen is not so much grey as blue; I see a sapphire tinge at the edges of it as it lies glassily still in its bottle. It is a version of a blue defined by *Chambers* – not 'the colour of the unclouded sky', but near to that of 'wood-smoke, skim-milk, lead'. It has a heavy oiliness about it, like good vodka. It is a mind-bending blue like the blue notes bent by fiddles in a tune like 'Rakish Paddy'. It is redolent with smoke and perfume:

> There's a neat little still at the foot of the hill
> Where the smoke curls up to the sky
> And by the smell you can plainly tell

That there's poteen, boys, close by
For it fills the air with a perfume rare
And 'twixt both me and you
As home we'll roll we drink a bowl
Or a bucketful of mountain dew

– although such olfactory advertisement of the product is hazardous.
For one of the big points in poteen is its very illicitness, and the
law is always thwarted by elaborate ritual.

Buying poteen in Glen—, we take a corkscrew brae down off
the main road. We go across a bridge and up a lane into the haggard
of a farm. We knock at the back door. A curtain is drawn back and
drawn again. The door opens and we go into the kitchen. Phatic
greetings are exchanged as the poteen-maker puts the kettle on for
tea. The talk is of the weather or the price of grass-seed as the
kettle begins to whistle up its blue steam. The pot is scalded. Tea
is made. Then the tea has to draw. More small talk, till 'I suppose
you'll be wanting a bag of them spuds', and we're brought out to
the yard again, and we climb these stone steps – are these 'The
Stony Steps' of the eponymous reel? – to the upper storey of a
barn, where there are spuds and poteen. He takes four bottles
of the 'Special Powers' and carefully clunks them into the earthy
dark of a spud-bag. Payment is made casually with a near-invisible
gesture of the wrist, taken casually and stuffed into a hip pocket.
More small talk before we're off.

In moonshine films the clientele appear to gather at obscure
crossroads and when they drink the stuff they do it out of
wide-necked glass receptacles – the 'Mason jars' of American
legend – which appear from the 'trunks' of 'automobiles', reminding
us how atavistic are Americans, with their quaint old-fashioned
terminologies like 'fall' and 'sidewalk'. It reminds me, curiously,
how 'Coke' is, in the Southern States, a generic term for 'pop' or
what they call a 'soda' in Yankeeland, whereas in Belfast soda is a farl
of bread; hence anyone named Farrell will get 'Soda' as a nickname.
There was a Soda Farrell who played hurling for Rossa . . . but I
digress. Back in America I remember how in semi-dry states, where
only beer was on sale in bars, people would go 'brown-baggin'':
that is, buying a fifth or a flat pint of Wild Turkey or Rebel Yell
or Early Times or whatever in a liquor store where you were served
from behind a grille and you felt like a criminal or a Securicor guard,

implicated in some complicated plot, and you brought it to the bar and placed it under your table still in its brown bag, since this was its cloak of invisibility. A blind eye was turned to things. I went 'brown-baggin'' myself in The Red Lion Inn just out of Winston-Salem on the road to Sodom or Intercourse or another of those bizarre North Carolina towns. Persuaded by my minders and the contents of the bag, I borrowed a guitar and entered the Saturday night Country and Western competition. I sang:

> For love and porter makes a young man older
> And love and whiskey makes him old and grey
> But what can't be cured, love, must be endured, love
> So now I'm off to Amerikay

That I won the first prize – a case of Pabst Blue Ribbon beer – was down, I think, to my Irish accent and some good ole Southern hospitality. That the brown bag is a camouflage or token of illegality brings me back to the subterfuge of tea in poteen and to how tea is used to stain boxwood flutes to make them look old, and of the rascally proximity of tea and poteen:

> For the dalin' men from Crossmaglen
> Put whiskey in me tay . . .

and in country houses poteen is still sometimes drunk from mugs, like tea, or from bowls, for that matter. And in days not so bygone, they ladled it out from churns or petrol drums, before the current custom of decanting it into mineral water bottles, mineral water not being Perrier nor Ballygowan, but pop or soda: what we in Belfast called 'lemonade' when I was young, and the Lemonade Man from Cantrell & Cochrane's or The Belfast Aerated Water Company came round in his clinking lorry and unloaded us some bottles of Orangeade or Attaboy. Lemonade – specific, not generic – came in two versions, brown and white; the brown, in the South of Ireland or The Republic or The Dear Old Free State or Eire, is known as Red Lemonade. So, these days, mineral water bottles contain poteen masquerading as White Lemonade; or such, at least, may have been the original rationale, for you do get poteen in inappropriate receptacles like Raspberryade.

And, of course, the bottle is a kind of brand name, advertising which locality the poteen was distilled in. Back in Winston-Salem on another trip, I remember a camp-follower of the Irish-American or American-Irish band Touchstone, whom I'd met in circumstances too complicated to be detailed here, produced a magic bottle of poteen. There is a ritual of tasting poteen which is mostly all the same, no matter if the stuff is good or bad. Except if it is really bad, in which case you spit it out. It takes the form of rare Scotch malt sniffing and sipping and rolling it around the palate, till you say, 'Quare stuff', and the guy then pours you a generous glug of it. So I did this thing, and said, 'Mmmmm, seems to have a hint of glen or bog about it, some kind of Northern tang', and identified it as a Glens of Antrim poteen. The camp-follower was impressed, and I hadn't the heart to tell her that the bottle's label – 'Braid Valley Mineral Water Company' – had revealed all. So then we all ended up at this great party in a librarian's house as high as kites and sat down in the kitchen where we played 'The Skylark' an unprecedented eighteen times. 'That poteen was quare stuff'.

Even Parliament whiskey has its rituals. 'Sailing Homewards from Rathlin Island', as the song has it, we once were introduced to a hitherto-unknown (to us) procedural detail, as, the morning after the night before, the boatman unscrewed a half-bottle of Bushmills, crushed the cap between finger and thumb, and threw it into the grey turbulent Sea of Moyle – 'Silent, O Moyle, be the flow of thy waters' – as token that the bottle would be drunk by us before we reached the harbour. This is a form of 'crack', or social exchange, and the humours of whiskey take many disguises.

The Mountain Road

This is a footnote to the foregoing, for after writing it I encountered moonshine on 24 February 1995 in the town of Hickory, North Carolina. I was appearing in The Bear's Lair as part of 'An Evening of Irish Poetry and Folk Music'; the other part was a band called The Celtic Folkers. The organiser, Rand Brandeis, had called me earlier in Belfast, asking if I had any special requirements, and I had jokingly asked for a little moonshine.

The night itself is moonlit, starry, frosty, and I'm standing outside The Bear's Lair smoking a cigarette when the connection is made. I am introduced to the moonshine people and two Mason jars appear:

> Got something here for ya.
> Clear white.
> This here's the apple brandy . . .
> and this here's the pear.
> Aged for four years.
> Yessir.
> Clear white. Cle-a-a-r Whi-i-i-te.
> Now you drink all you like.
> You drink your fill.

I unscrew the lid from the preserve jar – and what is 'clear white' but a preserve? – and take a tentative sip. I experience the oxymoron, 'firewater'. It is like and not like poteen. It has a lucid sting on the lips, a zigzag burning trickle down the throat. It has a certain *je ne sais quoi* like that of the *eaux-de-vie* I tasted in Brittany – *eau-de-vie de poire, de fraise, de pruneau.* Now that I remember it, I had asked for *un esprit très fort*, and was disconcerted by the laughter of the landlady, not knowing, then, that I had asked for a strong ghost: the English language, with its layered almost-synonyms, had inspired me into bad French. But the strong ghosts were doled out in tiny modicums, and I had to ask her, *très très grand*, till she poured me what I considered a respectable double slug. So I ran the gamut of the *eaux-de-vie*. Later in the trip, Job Nedellec (aptly-named from the Breton for Xmas) presented me with a litre of his uncle's *lambic*; that is, 'still', as we would call it, a version of 'alembic', from the Arabic, *Al Anbiq*, a still. This is a form of cider brandy – better, to my mind, than commercial Calvados; it is the best home distillate I have ever tasted, with a curious magic mushroom tang to it, that got you high and clear and focussed in on what you thought you might be at.

Back in The Bear's Lair, and forward many years in time, I have imbibed a bit of moonshine and I'm listening to The Celtic Folkers. The fiddle-player has been introduced to me as Fred Lail and he has a Carolinian accent you could cut with a Bowie knife, but he is playing this graceful bouncy Irish music and I'm trying to put my finger on it – the set of tunes, the way he bows them and the way he holds himself – till it strikes me that he mentioned he knew the playing of James Kelly, the Irish fiddler now resident in Miami. And now I can see James in the way Fred sits, how he leans into the tune at some crucial point with a gesture of the shoulder and head, how he signals the onset of the next tune in the series with a dainty semi-pirouette of the foot raised off the ground, as if he made a bracket or a comma.

I am so taken by this *doppelgänger* vision that I go up and whisper 'James Kelly' in his ear just as the set is coming to a close. 'You have James to a T', I say. Fred is pleased as a jug of punch, and so am I, for it turns out that hearing James play was what started him off, and we both love James' playing. We go through a litany of other names: Fred Finn, Peter Horan, Bobby Casey, Patrick Helly – signposts or guides through a terrain we have both explored from our very different necks of the woods, and yet have stumbled on the same nexuses.

But their names and the names of tunes we delineate the interdigitations of the music and its players; we form an instant kinship through a repertoire as we recite its genealogy. At the end of the night we play 'The Mountain Road' about twenty-something times for the sheer joy and hell of it, and because it's a good, well-constructed tune that bears playing again and again. Each time round we find another nuance, another way of going off the metronome while keeping to the wavy underlying beat, and after so many times you lose count of them. There is no chronological time, because the tune invents its own dimensions. The mountain road winds up and up in ornamental gradients, each twist with yet another view: so many zigzags, till you hit the plateau and you see how far this road extends; now you're on a steady rolling level, it's as if the road is taking you, not you taking it. It's a buzz like that endorphin high of cyclists as they push themselves through the wall of pain and hardship, and come out the other end relaxed and synchronised; they are tuned-in to the bike, and its rhythm has become a biorhythm. Miles of time go by in less time than it takes to tell.

Eight days later, I'm in Montreal. By some other labyrinthine nexus, I end up at a party where, among a good few very good musicians, I meet a Montrealer fiddler of Armenian stock, David Papazian. We go through the usual establishment of stock tunes to play, and realise, as we go on, that the stock is getting larger. Meeting another musician for the first time is an elaborate encounter: a cat-and-mouse game, a courting ritual, or an exchange of phatic gifts. Ground rules are drawn up. It is a kind of poker, trying to suss out the other's hand, and whether he has any wild cards up his sleeve. We work out suits or suites or sets of tunes. And it seems whatever I play, Papazian can play too; if not, he picks it up the second or third time round. He is, as they say, 'quick to lift a tune'. Happily compatible, we take a break and smoke:

> The moment of taking a cigarette allows one to open a parenthesis in the time of ordinary experience, a space and time of heightened attention that gives rise to a feeling of transcendence, evoked through the ritual of fire, smoke, cinder connecting hands, lungs, breath and mouth. It produces a little rush of infinity that alters perspectives, however slightly, and permits, albeit briefly, an ecstatic standing outside of oneself.
>
> Richard Klein, *Cigarettes are Sublime*

And of course music does that too, and we move between two transcendental states like we are off the planet, gazing at the lucid constellations as we say their names: Peter Horan, Deirdre Hevlin, Jim McGrath, John Kennedy, Denis Sweeney, Andy Dickson: a different astrology from that explored in Hickory, but one which intersects it, like Libra carried on the shoulders of Orion. We can now glimpse the future of our tunes, and what we'll play with what, and what will be the time to play them, for we now have stacks of time.

I'm smoking roll-up cigarettes which, unlike saltpetre-packed commercial fags, go out when you stop smoking them. I roll one, take a puff or two before Papazian springs another tune on me. I put it down. I re-ignite it briefly in the lull between a set and put it down again; and so on, till I make one roll-up last an elongated hour. If time is a dimension, it is disturbed by these hyphenated pauses and by the way that jigs and reels are played in different times at different times. It is totally confused by slides and polkas. And I'm a moving present dot between the shifting staves of past and future. I open the pinched-up foil packet of Old Holborn and take out a right-hand thumb-and-finger pinch of it, while my left hand in its automatic pilot mode holds out the prepared paper in a tripod thumb and two fingers. I tease the tobacco out across the length of Rizla paper, and remember briefly how tobacco – 'snout', as they call it – is a currency in prison, where there is lots of time, and where cigarettes can have a bearing on the time allotted.

So I put the roll-up to my lips left-handedly, while my right is poised with its pink plastic lighter and I feel the callus on my thumb prepared to strike its eternal flint-wheel. I light up. I inhale. Papazian starts up another tune. He holds his lit Player's Medium between the first and second fingers of his bow hand as he bows the tune, until the growing residue of ash becomes the length of a pinky fingertip and furls off gently to crash noiselessly on the scurf of rosin sedimented on the belly of the fiddle. He plays the tune another time or two until the cigarette is dead. It is a mode of secondary smoking, where the line of smoke is wafting randomly between the rolls and triplets and its longitude is wavered as the mean time of the fiddle-bow takes the future on, and plays with it. He stops and flicks the dead stub to the floor. It is discarded like an accidental grace-note, or a blip of secondary time that underlies the tune. He takes a sip of transcendental whiskey.

The Hurler on the Ditch

I took my first drink of whiskey in an upstairs lounge in Cork City. I shut my eyes and sip, and see its gold glint quiver in the glass. I didn't like it, I remember, and swapped it for a team-mate's glass of Double. We were three boys, colleagues in the County Antrim Minor (under-18) hurling team and we were down to contest the All-Ireland Semi-final of 1965. As it turned out, we were devastated by superior opposition, and what little I remember of the match has to do with time.

Back at home, I could gauge to a nicety when to hold back and then accelerate in order to get my hand to the low ball down the wing. I soon discovered that the Cork boys worked to a different tempo: I confidently reached out for the first such ball that came my way, and found my knuckles nearly taken off by the blade of my marker's hurley; they played to different rules as well, it seemed, and this was fair game.

Autres temps, autres moeurs: in hurling, as in most games, time is crucial; it is what you have to find or make, for time will give you space in which to act. Because of the reach of the hurley-stick extended in your hand, the effective tackling distance can be as much as eight or nine feet, especially if you 'hook' an opponent's stick (i.e. tackle from behind, a perfectly legitimate move). So, much thought and practice is devoted to the strategy of space and time: feints, side-steps, 'shortening' the stick, little half-flicks (what they'd call a 'bunt' in baseball), swerves and jinks; any hurler worth the name will have a repertoire of these. It has been reckoned that you need some eighty different separate skills in hurling – each might be learned separately, or in conjunction with others, but all must be allied finally and bonded in a programmed schema.

A situation will present itself which you recall subconsciously:

you recognise its shape as if it were a tune in three dimensions –
no, in four – and you fit it up against whatever combination was
deployed the last time round, and tinker instantaneously, making
necessary readjustments in the light of that split second. The chink
you waltz through opens up a gap. You find another version of the
move, and an almost-florid run of notes comes out unflurried in a
tune you thought you knew, but realise, now, how one-dimensional
your musicology had been: it is as if there were a new slant to the
autumn sunshine of your neighbourhood, and your feet scuffle
through the crisp fallen leaves in dance-step patterns.

In American football, the running-back will try to run at a
predetermined angle through an ideal space created for him by
his line-men. That space, in actuality, is up for grabs, and it's
the job of the opposing line to break it up, unstitch it and throw
the runner out of kilter. As the big chefs in the steaming kitchen
of the scrimmage grunt and heave against each other, spoiling one
another's broth and slapping one another with their arms like hams,
this black cat of a running-back darts underneath their feet, and,
in a zigzag burst of inspiration, his boots discover new peripheries
of vision. Eventually, some three or four yards later, he is stopped,
and, falling, twists in some new stunt in his acrobatic nine lives, and
earns the extra yard. This is a gorgeous management of time, where
tiny semidemiquavers are perceived to change the standard pattern
of the reel. They line up once again, this time in a new formation,
poised, immobile till the ball is 'snapped'; and like a greyhound
from its trap, another running-back emerges almost horizontally.
The pattern kaleidoscopes again.

I believe that American kids take their footballs and their baseball
mitts to bed with them. I used to take my hurley-stick to bed. I
took it everywhere with me, whenever possible. Running messages,
I remember cold crisp winter evenings of early dusk: I'd take the
stick and ball with me and juggle them in some imagined saga of
a match until I reached the chemist's shop. I'd pause outside its
lighted cornucopia of Christmas-packaged baby soaps and shaving
kits, its neon signatures of perfume, my breath misting on the glass.
Inside would be the half-time interlude, a space to recollect and plan
amidst the smell of gauze and liniment and sticking-plaster.

I'd buy the packet of 7 O'Clock razor blades for my father and
come running out wound-up for the second half (or rather, 'the
penultimate moiety', as the old-style sports writers called it) of

the brilliant game where I was Jimmy Doyle, and in the last split second, before I swerved through the front garden gate, I'd score the winning goal by hitting, with a satisfying clang, the corrugated zinc dustbin parked in the driveway (or the side path, as we called it, since we didn't have a car). The whole half took about three minutes, from shop to home base. Without a stick and ball, the run might take fifty seconds: the extra time was taken up by fouls, frees, and taking passes from the rebound off garden walls. The beauty of it was, if you didn't get it right the first time, you could have an instant replay where you did. You made your own time.

Day in, day out, I would practise. Our family moved from the Lower Falls to a semi-detached housing estate in Andersonstown when I was about seven. Our street, Mooreland Drive, was a cul-de-sac which abutted on the side wall of Roger Casement Park, the main GAA (Gaelic Athletic Association) ground in County Antrim, where all the big games were played. The wall had two big sheet-iron green-painted gates (always locked, except for really big matches) which each had eight riveted panels; the two gates, together, were about the same dimensions as a goal-mouth. I had read that Jimmy Doyle, the great Tipperary forward of the Sixties, used to practise by hitting the ball through the rungs of a ladder. I used to imagine receiving the ball from an imaginary team-mate with my back to goal, turning quickly, and shooting at a nominated panel (I had given them mental numbers). Or, facing goal, I'd practise frees, and try to hit a line of rivets and anticipate the unpredictable rebound. Sometimes, I would miss entirely, and the ball would soar over the gate and get lost in the long grass on the back of the embankment round the pitch. I'd climb over. Sometimes I would find the ball, and sometimes not; and sometimes, I would stumble, literally, on a ball I'd lost a year or two ago. I used old tennis balls for practice: exhumed from their damp grassy tangled catacombs, they'd come out with a slow reluctant rip, their fuzz all mouldering and rotted to the bare black rubber. I was an archaeologist of my own past.

Day in, day out, I wasn't always on my own. The two small streets of Mooreland Drive and Mooreland Park provided quite a few county players: the Crossey brothers, the Denny brothers, the Heenans, and myself. The sound of the puck of a ball was a summons. Within a minute or two of coming out on the street I might be joined by John Crossey, for example, who was a few years younger, but possessed a natural gift for the game, and from whom I learned more, in those early years, than I did from anyone else. Our conversation was minimal and if I met him now, I wouldn't know what to say to him; our crack was the way you made a fancy drop-shot, or blocked a fast ball hit directly at you, or casually 'doubled' on a high ball. At other times, the little cul-de-sac became a vast arena, with marathon games played well past lighting-up time, and you went by guess-work, imagining the play the way you would in a Spot-the-Ball competition. It was good training, since 'reading' the play – anticipating the ball by a holistic vision of the other players' movements – is an essential skill, just as music players read each other's body language.

I stopped hurling many years ago, but dream recurrently of hurling to this day. It is usually a nightmare of incompetence. I fumble, stumble, I am half-blind. My hands feel like asbestos gloves. I have no touch. I make Freudian slips. The playing field is a morass with cattle stranded in it, lowing mournfully; or else it is a quarry suddenly invaded by machine-gun-toting factions of a minor revolution. The hurley is of teaspoon size and shape; the ball is a balloon. There are many annexes and versions of this dream, and I am waiting for the night when everything will turn out right, and the dream will bear some semblance of a past reality.

It is snowing lightly in reality; it is almost dark. The air is blue-grey, violet. It stings like aftershave. The hurley is a flexible extension of my hands, my wrists, my eyes. I strike the ball for the hundredth time, registering the slight 'pock' as it meets the sweet spot of the stick. My body is weightless, and I leave no footprints on the freshly-fallen snow. I watch the ball drift through the cold clean dusk. It strikes the iron gate and quivers with a faint reverberation, then it spins back lazily. I see its S-line curving towards my outstretched hand. I've been out here for hours, but yesterday, tomorrow, do not exist. There is no time. There's only this.

Nor am I alone: I have imagined crowds and team-mates and an opposition. I am like the poteen-stricken fiddler who stumbles into the ruined house one night and tells of the great *ceili* he made, not knowing he'd communicated with the dead.

Johnny Going to Ceili

I learned 'Johnny Going to _Ceili_', together with the other tunes
in the set, 'The Long Slender Sally' and 'The Gossoon that Beat
His Father', from Cathal McConnell of Bellanaleck on the shores
of Lough Erne; and I think Cathal learned them from the late
John Maguire, father of the fiddle maestro Sean McGuire [sic],
and I couldn't tell you where John got them. However, it's not
their provenance I want to discuss here, but the notion of a _ceili_.

In my teens in Belfast, a _ceili_ was a social event imprimatured
by the Catholic Church where boys and girls met each other
under close sacerdotal supervision and practised mimimal-contact
dancing; the best part was where you got to swing the girl. The
only drinks were soft, though some boys were known to smuggle
in flat half-bottles of 'British Wine'. It was a far cry from the _ceili_
I encountered later on in life. One version of it goes like this:

Ceili

If there was a house with three girls in it,
It only took three boys to make a dance.
You'd see a glimmer where McKeown's once was
And follow it till it became a house.
But maybe they'd have gone on, up the hill
To Loughran's, or made across the grazing,
Somewhere else. All those twistings and turnings,
Crossroads and dirt roads and skittery lanes:
You'd be glad to get in from the dark.

And when you did get in, there'd be a power
Of _poitín_. A big tin creamery churn,

A ladle, those mugs with blue and white bars.
Oh, good and clear like the best of water.
The music would start up. This one ould boy
Would sit by the fire and rosin away,
Sawing and sawing till it fell like snow.
That *poitín* was quare stuff. At the end of
The night you might be fiddling with no bow.

When everyone was ready, out would come
The tin of Tate and Lyle's Golden Syrup,
A spoon or a knife, a big farl of bread.
Some of those same boys wouldn't bother with
The way you were supposed to screw it up.
There might be courting going on outside,
Whisperings and cacklings in the barnyard;
A spider thread of gold-thin syrup
Trailed out across the glowing kitchen tiles
Into the night of promises, or broken promises.

Much of that poem is taken from the talk of the late John Loughran, fiddle-player, singer, raconteur, and frequenter of many's the *ceili*: labyrinthine, funny, scatty, precise, scathing talk that mixed modes and genres in the way *ceili*-ing itself did.

In its primary sense, *ceili* does not necessarily include music. Father Dinneen's *Irish Dictionary* has 'an evening visit, a friendly call', with 'an evening of musical entertainment' secondary, and that probably in deference to those evenings formally devised by the early Gaelic League. The word derives from *céile*, 'a companion'. Dinneen's entry is a full column long, and the word is used in conjunction with others to represent various shades of identity or contrariness. *Fear chéile* is a husband, *bean chéile*, a wife, which seem to be archaic equivalents of the modern, politically-correct 'partner' (at the time of writing; no doubt other compromises will appear). I recall a London-Irish band of the Sixties known as *Le Chéile*, which could be translated as 'together' or 'ensemble' or 'in concert'.

Anyway, in rural areas, *ceili* denotes a visit or a series of visits; a way of passing the time of day or night. Anglicised as *kayley*, it is current in West Ulster, especially, sometimes as a verb – recalling an absent friend, one might say, 'I used to kayley with him'. Before wireless and television, the *ceili* was a *samizdat* of sorts, a news-and-scandal channel, or communications network. One boy might call and make his *ceili* with his mate down the loaning; then the pair of them might carry on to someone else's house. Others would be at the same thing. All around the townland shadows flit between the scattered lighted houses, until, late on in the evening, they converge on one house pre-arranged among themselves, or authorised by custom. Then indeed there might be music, dancing, eating, drinking, talking, or the making of 'spakes' – pithy statements, verbal stratagems, elaborate hedge-school nonsense – or the throwing out of 'guesses' or riddles.

Such culminations, *ceilis* or parties and their local variations are known under different names in different parts: 'time', 'do', 'hooley', 'night', *oíche áirneála, scoraíocht,* (from *scor,* to share, cognate with English shear, sheer, etc.), 'spree', 'rake' (in parts of West Tyrone) and so on. Around Coolea in West Cork, they talk of 'capers'; and lately, the term has been extended to mean 'dope' or 'blow'; liquid caper, or tetrahydrocannabinol, is known as 'Oil of Coolea'. An interesting offshoot is the Anglo-Irish 'coshery', meaning, according to *Chambers,* 'the ancient right of an Irish chief to quarter himself and his retainers on his tenantry', from the Irish *cóisir* (pronounced 'kosher'), 'a feast, a festive party; a wedding party, esp. *en route,* escorting the bride to the place of the feast'. This, I think, must come from the English 'coach', which in turn comes from the Hungarian town of Kocs; and its first recorded use in 1556 suggests the notion isn't all that ancient. It sounds like good crack anyway.

Which brings us to the famous 'crack', popularly and recently Gaelicised as *craic* and advertised in countless retro-renovated bars throughout the land, as in 'Live *Ceol,* Sandwiches and *Craic*'. Non-Irish speakers in particular will insist on its ancient Gaelic lineage and will laboriously enunciate this shibboleth to foreigners who take it for a pharmacological rather than a social high. In fact, the *Oxford English Dictionary* dates crack, 'chat, talk of the news', to 1450. 'Cracker' is 'one who or that which cracks, esp. a boaster, a liar', reminding me of the Fermanagh use of 'lie', meaning an impressively convincing tall story, or wind-up. As the late Eddie Duffy, flute-player and cracker, would say, 'The trouble with the young ones nowadays, they can play none, they can sing none, they can dance none, and they can tell no lies.' In Belfast dialect, a cracker is a thing which is the best of its kind, a superlative. A good-looking woman is 'a real cracker'. The Belfast comedian Frank Carson (no relation), in the middle of whatever routine applause, would come out with his catch-phrase, 'It's a cracker!'

It seems to me that 'crack' was, until fairly recently, confined to the North of Ireland, for I remember Southerners would look somewhat nonplussed at our coming out with, 'The crack was ninety' about an especially good session, or simply, 'It was great crack'. They were similarly confused by our expression, 'How's about ye?' for 'How are you' or 'Hello', reminding me of the terse Derry greeting, 'Yes'. This, depending on inflection, has a gamut of nuances, especially when it precedes the name of the addressee, as in, 'Yes, Mote!' It can be welcoming, quizzical, contemplative or social. As Frank Carson's other catch-phrase goes, 'It's the way I tell 'em!'

It reminds me of a joke:

There was this Yank once,
came over on his holidays.
'Vacations', as they call them there.
And he stopped off at this bar in Connemara.
And you know the way you step from sunlight
into dark, you have to rub your eyes
before you see, and then you see
this row of men with hats and raincoats on,
all sitting at the bar.
And it's deadly quiet. Not a word from anyone.
And the Yank orders a pint.
And the pint's just settled, and he's put it to his lips,
And someone says, 'Twenty-three.'
And everyone cracks up at this.
They slap their trouser-knees
They think this number is hilarious.
Then there's quiet once again.
A while goes by, then someone says, 'Eleven hundred and nine.'
And everyone cracks up at this as well.
And this goes on, these guys calling numbers out.
And some get great response,
and others not so much.
So the Yank is watching all of this,
not knowing what to make of it.

So he asks the barman what's going on.
And the barman says, 'Well, it's like this:
these men you see are going on a long time.
They've been drinking here these fifty years, if a day.
And, you know, they have their jokes all off.
And they have them in a sort of mental catalogue.
So to save the time of telling it,
they just call out the number.'
And the Yank thinks this is great crack altogether,
and he says, 'Say, do you think I could have a go?'
And the barman says, 'Be my guest.'
So the Yank calls out, 'One hun'red an' forty-four!'
And there's silence.
So he tries another number. 'Sevenny-one!'
And there's silence.
And he tries all the numbers he knows.
And there's still silence.
So he goes up to the barman, and he says, 'I've tried,'
he says, 'all the numbers I know,
and no-one's laughing.'
And the barman looks at him, and says,
'Well, sir, it's not the joke, you see.
It's the way you tell 'em.'

Dowd's No. 9

I last played the reel 'Dowd's No. 9' along with James Kelly, the Dublin fiddle-player now resident in Miami, who was then back for a month or so for a short tour of Ireland. We were sitting at the kitchen table I'm typing at right now and some discussion of the tune arose, whose thread I've since lost. So I decide to phone James in Miami, only to discover I've lost the number. Deirdre suggests I phone Len Graham, who is bound to have the number. I phone Len in Mullaghbawn, and Len tells me that James is back in Ireland, doing work at some recording studio in Clare. I ring the number he gives me, but there's no reply. Deirdre suggests I ring Joe McElheran. So I phone my box-playing brother-in-law Joe, who doesn't know the tune but suggests his fiddle-playing partner Denis Sweeney might.

It turns out Denis is the very man to tell me who Dowd might have been. The tune, he tells me, was recorded in the Forties by the Donegal fiddler Hugh Gillespie, who, Denis thinks, quite possibly got it from Michael Coleman, so that would date it to the Twenties at least. Denis reckons the name is more properly O'Dowd, who was a Sligo fiddler of Coleman's generation. We speculate a little as to what happened to Nos. 1–8 and whether there were more in the series. Whatever the case, whether he lost them one night when on the rake, they are lost to the tradition; maybe they just didn't stick or maybe the title is an elaborate joke. Then there's 'Dowd's Favourite', which has some modal kinship to 'No. 9', and Denis lilts a bit of it over the phone to me, putting me in mind of 'The Telephone Reel' which Gary Hastings got on the phone from Cathal McConnell, from whose playing and that of Peg McGrath I first heard 'Dowd's No. 9' on a tape that Gary got from Maura McConnell and which Gary loaned me (people had no copying facilities in those days). So I start lilting 'Dowd's No. 9' through the phone to Denis, and Denis says, 'Naw, this is the way she goes,' and lilts me this other reel with a similar but different structure, which is indeed the tune I played with James Kelly, but what I had in my mind tonight was, I think, the one it's paired with on the tape. It's an understandable labyrinth – these lateral slips give one clue as to how tunes acquire their 'aka's.

And now I see the tape in my mind's eye, with Maura's blue looped ballpoint writing on it, and I'm about to go and look for it, till I remember that each time I go to look for it, I realise I've given it back. And yet its ghostly presence hovers on, and I can see the open drawer it's supposed to be in, together with those orphan cassettes with no cases, for cassette and case bear the same relationship as a pair of socks, of which one is bound to get lost in the wash.

I hear snatches of the tape, fragments floating up from archaeologies of previous hearings, and I can hear Cathal and Peg and Kathleen Smith who was there too, and the funny repetitive circular structure of 'Dowd's No. 9'. I see them sitting in the McConnells' kitchen in Toneyloman near Bellanaleck in County Fermanagh, and I can see McConnell's strong square-tipped fingers holding the flute left-handed, then there's a lull – desultory talk of tunes, and clinking teacups – and then McConnell has gone off on some other musical tangent hinted to him by 'No. 9'.

Travelling with Cathal McConnell, or meeting him on some rare occasion when he calls into the house and makes a *ceili*, I have often been amazed by his propensity for tunes, his memory for the words of songs, and his ability to link them in a vast cartography of time and place, a map of many layers through which Cathal slips and visits, time and time again, and brings back strange new tunes and news, as if he were invisible:

Invisibility, let me explain, gives one a slightly different sense of time; you're never quite on the beat . . . Instead of the swift and imperceptible flowing of time, you are aware of its nodes, those points whose time stands still or from which it leaps ahead. And you slip into the breaks and look around.

Ralph Ellison, *Invisible Man*

That reminds me of McConnell's funny beat, the way he pushes the tune forward and plays reels in a kind of staccato Highland way at times. And each tune has a catalogue of variations within the time, and genealogies of memory, so that the huge ornate system can be entered anywhere, for any point will lead you to a destination or a halt *en route* that might prove more interesting than what you thought you might be looking for. This is the classical memory system, as outlined by Aristotle:

> Generally speaking the middle point seems to be a good point to start from; for one will recollect when one comes to this point, if not before, or else one will not recollect from any other. For instance, suppose one were thinking of a series, which may be represented by the letters ABCDEFGH; if one does not recall what is wanted at E, yet one does at H; from that point it is possible to travel in either direction, that is either towards D or towards F. Suppose one is seeking for either G or F, one will recollect on arriving at C, if one wants G or F. If not then on arrival at A. Success is always achieved in this way. Sometimes it is possible to recall what we seek and sometimes not; the reason being that it is possible to travel from the same starting-point in more than one direction; for instance from C we may go directly to F or only to D.
>
> Aristotle, *De Memoria et Reminiscentia*

So Cathal flits among the alphabet of musical encounters, summoning up the living and the dead. This is a space of fractal variation, where the line representing a coastline on the Ordnance map is, in reality, an ornate stretch of complicated interdigitation:

> 'Interdigitation' is the fine term I overhear the scientists using for the way in which one natural zone meets another along a complex boundary of salients and re-entrants; the close-set come-and-go of its syllables is almost enough to convey the word's meaning, but etymologically it is a little inadequate to such cases as this Connemara coastline where land and sea not only entwine their crooked fingers but each element abandons particles of itself temporarily or permanently to the clutch of the other.
>
> Tim Robinson, *Setting Foot on the Shores of Connemara*

So it is with complicated interdigitations of tunes, six fingers on the flute describing shades of space and rhythm. 'Hugh Gunn would have played it this way, but then his nephew Big John put another turn in it.' The tune becomes a family tree. It is a conversation piece, a *modus operandi*, a way of renegotiating lost time. Our knowledge of the past is changed each time we hear it; our present time, imbued with yesterday, comes out with bent dimensions. Slipping in and out of nodes of time, we find our circles sometimes intersect with others. Yet there is a wider circle we can only dimly comprehend, whose congregation is uncountable, whose brains and hands have shaped this tune in ways unknowable to us. We do not know how far or deep its palimpsests extend. We do not even know O'Dowd, or whether he made up the tune, or simply borrowed it and thought he made it up.

But the tune has been passed to us by a series of invisible and visible presences, and we like to think of the man who made it or purloined it or dreamed it up. So I imagine O'Dowd in a slouch hat and a gaberdine, extracting a Player's No. 6 from its packet of ten. He has just played 'No. 9'. In fact, he's just come from the fiddle competition where he witnessed some new boy playing 'Dowd's No. 9', and getting nowhere, for it is indeed *the way you play them* that's important.

And other kinds of numbers are important to the competition or the *fleadh*.

The Standard

1. There is no standard.

2. *Marking Scheme*

Style and Ornamentation	45
Quality of Voice	15
Quality and Choice of Song	10
Phrasing and Clarity	10
Rhythm	10
Interpretation and Expression	10
TOTAL	100

Comhaltas Ceoltóirí Éireann
Guide to Adjudication, 1969

3. Deirdre and I have made a tape for my brother Pat, who plays the melodeon. We call it *Standard Tunes* because they are standard to us and to many of our generation; but when we play them out, these days, they are perceived by some as old and strange.

4. *Ged a chual' iad an ceòl, cha do thuig iad am port* –
Though they heard the music, they didn't get the tune.

Gaelic Proverb

5. I dislike the idea of a fully-keyed flute, such as the Radcliffe system played by the late Paddy Carty; but I love his music, and the flute is necessary to it.

6. . . . among traditional musicians nothing is so noticeable as the absence of uniformity of style or system.

Captain Francis O'Neill,
Irish Folk Music: A Fascinating Hobby, 1910

7. *Word-Meanings, Etc.*

It has been said already that in this style of singing a great deal depends on the exact meaning of the words and units of speech. They have precedence over the music, the latter having been composed for and allied to the words. The words should be sung as they might be well spoken. Correct interpretation will play an important part here. Proper inflection and intonation are also very important.

Comhaltas Ceoltóirí Éireann
Guide to Adjudication, 1969

8. There are innumerable standards.

9. There were these three fiddlers once upon a time.
And they were in for this competition.
And the first one came up
and he was dressed in a dress-suit
and he had a dicky-bow and bib on him.
And the fiddle-case was made out of crocodile skin.
And when he brought out the fiddle,
what was it, but a Stradivarius.
And he started to play,
and beGod, he was desperate.

And the second fiddler came up,
and he was wearing a nice Burton's suit
and a matching handkerchief and tie
and socks with clocks on them.
And he had a nice wooden case
and not a bad fiddle in it,
so he got it out and started to play,
and beGod, he was desperate.

And the third fiddler came up
and the elbows was out of his jacket
and the toes peeping from his shoes,
and the fiddle-case was tied with bits of wire
and when he brought out the fiddle,
there was more strings on the fiddle

than there was on the bow.
And he started to play.
And beGod, he was desperate too.

From the story-telling of Mick Hoy

10. There's many's a one can play the reels and jigs, but it's the slow air that'll sort them out.

Anonymous *Fleadh* pundit

11. *Ní féidir liom a rá céard é an sean-nós, ach aithním é nuair a chloisim é* – I couldn't tell you what the *sean-nós* is, but I know it when I hear it.

Anonymous *Fleadh* adjudicator

12. Dear Sir,
Concerning your letter which I received to-day as an acknowledgement of comments which I recently made in writing, in common with other members of the Organisation to which I have the honour to belong, I wish to further state as an ex-soldier of the Army which helped to achieve freedom for at least the major portion of this country, that I find it most galling to have to witness what I consider to be a gradual departure from cultural standards in the matter of musical entertainment towards the barbaric culture of the African jungle or the environment of the Red Indian Totem-pole by RTE over the years.

Open letter to Teilifís Éireann, 1969

13. Some years ago I was at a Masonic concert in a Connaught town. A man from London, where he had lived, perhaps, in some coterie where good taste protested against modern taste, sang a couple of old English folk-songs, but all the other songs were vulgar and modern. Instead of an ancient tradition, one found the short-lived conventions of this age, the insincerity, the shallow cleverness, the reeking vulgarity. I had never been at a concert of this kind before, and listened in astonishment. I knew many of the people there, but it had never occurred to me that they had tastes harder to forgive than any vice. Presently

somebody sang about whiskey and shillelaghs and Donnybrook fair, and all those Irish men and women applauded. I waited till my voice could be heard, and hissed loudly.

W.B. Yeats, *An Claidheamh Soluis*, 1901

14. And here's this great fiddle-player, Jane O'Doe. *91*. That speaks for itself. That is a good mark. It is a great mark. Rarely in the history of this competition has such a mark been achieved. But then here's this other fiddle-player, John O'Doe. And to show you how much better *he* was, here's his mark . . . *91½*.

Anonymous *Fleadh* adjudicator

15. Generally, music feedeth the disposition of spirit it findeth.

Francis Bacon, *Essays*

16. The perfectly placed voice is a mystic thing that floats on the breath like a celluloid ball on a jet of water. It is neither in the throat nor in the nose, but outside the lips, where it remains immovable.

'F. Sharp' (Faith Compton MacKenzie), *The Gramophone*

17. Deirdre was once asked to adjudicate the fiddle competition in the County —— *Fleadh*. Unfortunately, the event attracted no entrants; but the competition had to happen and a winner be selected. It so happened that Mr X, generally regarded as the best fiddle-player in the area, might well have gone in for it; however, he couldn't be got out of the pub, except for the official free high tea he felt it was his duty to attend. Deirdre was dispatched to the tea-room above the hall, and managed to inveigle Mr X into playing the requisite reel, jig and slow air, in between the soup, the salad sandwiches and the jelly trifle. He was then presented with an enormous trophy, much to his surprise.

18. From caution, rather than from necessity, we may add, that the beautiful in music is totally independent of *mathematics*.

Dr Eduard Hunslick, *The Beautiful in Music*, 1891

19. The bewildering variety of settings or versions of traditional Irish tunes is fully equalled by the confusing diversity of names by which many of them are known.

Captain Francis O'Neill,
Irish Folk Music: A Fascinating Hobby, 1910

20. . . . the melodies of many folk-songs are inherently of the very strongest, and demand proportionately strong treatment if due balance is to be preserved. There is no object in neglecting the results of the advance which music has made from the experience of centuries, when the utilisation of it will enhance their inherent qualities. A composer of the sixteenth century would not have used the style of Dunstable for such a purpose; nor would Stevenson, with his Haydnesque proclivities, serve as a pattern for an arranger of Irish melodies now.

Charles Villiers Stanford, *Musical Composition*, 1911

21. I remember as a small boy of about five lying on a heap of straw on the granary floor watching Grand-dad mend holes in an old corn-sack draped across his knee with a curved packing-needle threaded with twine that smelt like turpentine. I lay there watching and listening intently as the ancient story unfolded, for the old man was singing, in a deep, resonant voice, a song he had heard from his own grandfather when he had been my age. The dog curled up beside me in the hot morning sunshine that slanted in through the large, open double doorway feigned sleep. Only the twitching of an ear or an occasional half-hearted attempt to wag his tail when Grand-dad's voice swelled to a higher note gave away the fact that he was alive to all that was going on.

Bob Copper, *A Song For Every Season*, 1971

22. The notion that songs and singing do not change is, to be sure, a myth. Obviously so at the simplest level, for how could words or music fail to vary or the function of old songs stay exactly the same? A nice comment on a good singer implies the possibility of change while rejecting it: 'He neither put till nor tuk from'.

Hugh Shields, *Narrative Singing in Ireland*, 1993

23. Songs are composed of words. These words must be heard – clearly and distinctly. Only good use of the organs of speech – the tongue, the teeth, the lips – will ensure this. Where necessary, competitors should be generally advised in this regard.

CCE guide to adjudication

24. I was once present at a singing competition in the town of ——, in the province of ——. The adjudicators were the well-known singers Mr Y and Mr Z. The venue was the local Temperance Hall. The competition started rather late, as the adjudicators found it difficult to leave the nearby pub. They eventually arrived with a brown paper bag which they discreetly shared under the trestle table. At the finale, everyone was awarded medals. The adjudicators sang a duet. Everyone was happy. Everyone felt well-adjudicated.

25. I knew some who did well in traditional singing until their success prompted them to take lessons in voice production from common modern teachers in towns, and they could never sing Irish any more. The colour was completely gone from the voice, and the power to glide and make the complicated graces so dear to music.

Revd Dr Richard Henebry,
A Handbook of Irish Music, 1928

26. Born and brought up in an atmosphere of tradition, the professor [P.J. Griffith] remains unconvinced that an untaught traditional fiddler could give a tune a colour and keenness unattainable by the trained hand of an Irishman who appreciates the beauty of Irish melody. Some there be, however, including the writer and some of the professor's friends, who cannot acquiesce in this view unreservedly; for that peculiar undefinable something in the tone and swing of an Irish reel, for instance, is instinctive rather than acquired.

Captain Francis O'Neill,
Irish Minstrels and Musicians, 1913

27. 'Our country musicians are possessed of the talent of music and have in their minds the idea of the beautiful in it, but they cannot reproduce them, for they lack the technical means of doing so.' *Applause.* 'Were they reasonably educated they would produce a race of musicians worthy of our history. Again, we had those who believed that Irish music should be rendered in scales of unusual construction. Many scales existed in ancient times but, alas, those who could teach us have gone. Because a singer or player, through lack of technical means, sang or played with a total disregard of any correctness of intonation, that did not qualify them to claim that they were using a scale of unusual construction. The majority of them did not adhere to the accepted musical scale, not that they used any other form of scale, but that their ear being totally untrained, they involuntarily produced a music not in any one scale, but in an infinity of scales of impossible construction.' *Laughter and applause.*

Mr Darley then gave his violin recital of Irish airs.

Freeman's Journal, 21 October 1908

28. The modern system . . . with fixed tonal elements, generalises or conventionalises all meanings and gives none. Hence it is permanently out of tune. And that will explain the strained and agonised feeling of one with a good ear and instinct for human music who has to listen, say, to a modern violinist (to say nothing of pianists), ever hoping and ever disappointed in the hope that the performer will slide the finger the least bit up or down and make sense . . . and the best fiddling I ever heard was a reel, slashed off one day by a tramp player in William Street, Portlaw. For, though I have heard much music since, the indescribable dash and call of that reel are dancing in my ears yet.

Revd Dr Richard Henebry,
A Handbook of Irish Music, 1928

29. Blues is truth. Blues are not wrote. The Blues are lived.

Brownie McGhee

30. I find among these people commendable diligence only on musical instruments, on which they are incomparably more skilled than any nation I have seen. Their style is not, as on the British instruments to which we are accustomed, deliberate and solemn but quick and lively; nevertheless the sound is smooth and pleasant.

It is remarkable that, with such rapid fingerwork, the musical rhythm is maintained and that, by unfailingly disciplined art, the integrity of the tune is fully preserved through the ornate rhythms and the profusely intricate polyphony . . . They introduce and leave the rhythmic motifs so subtly, they play the tinkling sounds on the thinner strings above the sustained sound of the thicker strings so freely, they take such secret delight and caress [the strings] so sensuously, that the greatest part of their art seems to lie in veiling it, as if 'That which is concealed is bettered – art revealed is art shamed.' Thus it happens that those things which bring private and ineffable delight to people of subtle appreciation and sharp discernment, burden rather than delight the ears of those who, in spite of looking do not see and in spite of hearing do not understand; to unwilling listeners, fastidious things appear tedious and have a confused and disordered sound.

Giraldus Cambrensis, Topographica Hiberniae, 1185

31. Mrs Liam O'Dwyer of Ardgrooms, Casteltownbere (formerly Miss Nellie MacQuille of Grotnagross, Athea) won the Munster concertina championship at Kilmallock *Fleadh Cheoil*. A remarkable coincidence is that her son, Sean O'Dwyer, present All-Ireland hop, step and jump champion and record holder, who recently captained the Irish athletics team against Spain, has also this year won the Dublin and Leinster concertina-playing championships. Both mother and son will now be competing in the forthcoming All-Ireland *Fleadh Cheoil*.

Treoir, November–December 1971

It Goes as Follies

The first *locus* on the road to the *fleadh* was not Irish music *per se*, but our discovery of Bearnageeha School in Belfast (from the Irish, *bearna gaoithe*, 'windy gap'). Some one of us – Archie, Mackers or myself – had found an extra-mural brochure detailing classes in the usual subjects: pottery, car maintenance, painting, cookery and flower arrangement. Bearnageeha had an evening class in folk music. One of the teachers was John Bennet, one-time member of The Glen Folk Four, which might have been defunct even then; the other was Brian Connors, author of 'Sailing Homeward to Rathlin Island'. I don't know what Brian is doing now, but John has achieved a certain notoriety as the host of a morning phone-in request show on Radio Ulster, where he gets to chat up old dears and play comfort-blanket music. Whatever: possibly we didn't learn much from the class itself, but we met kindred spirits; we met Protestants.

The era – even then, I think we suspected that the Sixties was an era – was buzzing with scholastic wranglings of the various dichotomies: Beatles/Stones, Clancy Brothers/Dubliners, acoustic/electric. We folkies or young fogies looked down our ethnic noses at the likes of those who'd come out with 'I see Dave Clark's zipping up the charts', or demonstrate the gestures of the latest dance craze in the playground. If pop music entered into it at all, it was only as a marker, to show which side you were on: the Stones, for instance, had some street cred, since they weren't really pop at all, but 'rock' – no, 'rhythm 'n' blues' – and had covered or ripped off all these beat-up blues guys like John Lee Hooker. The Stones were rough; the Beatles, smooth. 'Serious music' critics drooled on in the London *Times* about the 'Schubertian cadences' of 'Eleanor Rigby' and the like: in our

99

eyes, they damned them with their fulsome praise, for our ideas of 'The Beautiful' in music took in some notions of a buzzy, grainy authenticity.

So, Mackers took the effete nylon strings off his guitar and put on steel; such was the effect of the increased tension that the belly lifted off the bottom in a matter of weeks. Then Mackers got this semi-acoustic guitar tailpiece somewhere and patched the guitar up and ran the steel strings down to the tailpiece, so it all looked really battered-up and lived-in, modified by accident and circumstance. And I borrowed a painful cheap steel-strung guitar – 'box', we used to call it then, whereas 'box' is now 'accordion' – with a terrible high action that left scars on your fingertips, and I learned how to play after a fashion. I got Pete Seeger's instructional LP, *How to Play the Folk Guitar*, from the Belfast Central Library. After weeks I learned the simple little finger-picking thing for 'Poor Howard':

> Poor Howard's dead and gone,
> Left me here to sing this song . . .

and it's like a mantra to me yet. I used to sit in the front room in the dusk playing it over and over till the black shiny vinyl was all scratched with its going back and back again and the letting down of the tone-arm and its needle cartridge with that little blip and crash between the dusty grooves.

It was the way I loved that chunky twelve-string run of Keith's on the Stones' 'Don't Play with Me, 'cos you're Playing with Fire'. It was the way I loved the grain and rhythm of Luke Kelly as he belted out 'The Rocky Road to Dublin', and I felt borne into a new dimension. It was the way I loved Leadbelly and believed in his romantic ex-con's story. It was the way I even loved Joan Baez.

As for Dylan, we *loved* Dylan. Dylan was the heir of Woody Guthrie, so we started to get into those chokey Dust Bowl ballads, and from thence into those doomy whiny bluesmen masters of the Mississippi Delta and Chicago: Blind Blake, Peetie Wheatstraw, Furry Lewis, Sleepy John Estes, Charlie Patton, Big Bill, Papa Charlie Jackson, Mississippi John Hurt, Frank Stokes, Peg-leg Howell, Jaybird Coleman, Blind Willie McTell, Rube Lacey, Skip James, Leroy Carr and Scrapper Blackwell, Memphis Minnie, Buddy Boy Hawkins, Sam Collins, Bo-weavil Jackson, Roosevelt

Sykes, Rambling Thomas, Blind Lemon Jefferson . . . the names swim up from the hiss and drizzle of re-mastered 78s as we sat in Mackers' gloomy front room in Albert Street, smoking Gallaher's Blues and admiring their iconic blue packet, our cigarette ends glowing redly in sporadic Morse as we deliberated on the various meanings of the universe. Bob summed it up like this:

> The keeper of the prison, he asked it of me
> How good, how good, does it feel to be free?
> And I answered him most mysteriously
> Are the birds free in the chains of their skyways?

I'm trying to retrace the chains and chains of footsteps on the road. We'd turn right at the Falls Road and take the hundred steps or so we walked so many times. I see a groove imprinted in the footpath, as if you could put a giant needle in it, and replay our overlapping conversations. Then into The Gladstone Bar: we loved its literal spit-and-sawdust, its parrot in a dangling cage, its gang of resident eccentrics who'd balance pints of 'British Wine' on their wine-stained caps and sing sentimental rebel songs until admonished by the gloomy barman. 'Pints o' wine! Pints o' wine!' the parrot shrieked. We'd drink pints of Single X with schooners of Mundies' sickly-sweet wine before staggering into the pouring night. From there we'd get the old No. 77 cross-town bus to the waterworks, and walk up the Antrim Road to Bearnageeha; or, as we heard of other venues, walk on down the Falls to The Spanish Rooms, or The Scrumpy Rooms, as they were fondly known for the fact that about 90 per cent of what was drunk there was cheap strong raw cider. Sometimes we'd take out a flagon of it (about ten shillings' worth, as I recall) as fuel for the session in Salisbury Street. Sometimes, we would fit another pub or two into the crawl: Kelly's Cellars, Hannigan's, The Washington, The Crown, The Boyne Bridge Tavern, even; Robinson's, beside The Crown, was a favourite adjunct on the way.

Robinson's had this unique booths structure that looked like a railway carriage running down the centre of the floor, with doors that opened up on either side, and little compartments that held six at a pinch; four was comfortable. It was perfect, since we knew that the mythology of trains and the blues were irrevocably entangled, or that trains could not be visualised without the sound-track of a gargled harmonica. 'Can't you hear that lonesome whistle blow?' And we believed that the technology of trains and cinema, historically, were linked, as the carriage windows framed a metronomic image-sequence, and the landscape flickered by as background to its narrative. This was one reason why so many films happened in trains: the train is a perfect vehicle for the plot; the train is cinema, and its linear construction – carriages, compartments, corridors and couplings – provides a diagram of narrative, where the spatial nodes between the carriages provide a focal point for subterfuge and the ground rushes past in the swaying chink beneath your feet. Here, the WC transcends its evacuatory role: it is a laboratory, not a lavatory, where twists and turns to the supposed main action are experimented with; where the murder weapon is concealed; where ticketless heroes evade conductors; where sudden couplings take place.

On trains in films the jacks is a spy-base, with dark-complexioned, suited men rushing in and out at furtive intervals in a Marx brothers routine. And somehow, time spent in the water-closet is a different time from that spent in the corridor, with its long panning shots that stare at people's faces as the hero or the anti-hero scans them, looking for a sign or code. This is high anxiety time, in which the time of the film is not advanced one jot, since nothing happens until it's time to happen; in contrast, the thunder-box advances time beyond the understanding of the characters who haven't been there. Meanwhile, a different time again is happening beyond the confines of the train, where presidents of Swiss banks and heroin conspirators have already outlined what their agents are supposed to know, or not.

And yet, the station or the destination cannot be the conclusion of the narrative, since everything is *en route*, and the smuggled tape will turn up somewhere else. They listen to it over and over, trying to make sense of hiss and drizzle. Long before that, someone was defenestrated from a train, but that was not important. For in films, an inordinate amount of people keep nearly missing trains, clinging almost horizontally to the rail so thoughtfully provided by the American Railroad Company, the way they rang their bells, decelerating into the isolated Prairies halt, where murder would be done, or retribution would occur; it was the way the wooden railroad bridge was burning, and the train ploughed through it, sometimes making it and sometimes not. Then the train would plunge and shriek, disintegrating, into this vast Grand Canyon of a gap, and sparks would fly.

Trainwreck was one device for getting rid of the baddies. They must have been bad baddies, for the good baddies held up trains and got away with it. They rode alongside trains on simultaneous horses, and jumped off them on to roofs of carriages, and overpowered the spatial nodes between the carriages until they jumped the engineer and fireman, and brought the train to a shuddering halt in the middle of this scrubby lot in Outer Hollywood. Strong-boxes would be blown up. Nervous passengers would proffer jewellery and watches, only to be refused, for these were noble baddies, driven into badness by some misdeed of the Civil War.

They were true Hoods or Pretty Boy Floyds or the James brothers, and they spoke for the American dream of the open road or railroad, for the railroad movie came before the road movie. Songs were made about them, and were sung in honky-tonk saloons where cowboys kept being taken upstairs. Buffaloes were shot in great abundance. Coolies sweated under straw hats. Poker was performed by cool dudes in black and white attire. Ladies' derringers appeared from handbags. Banks in border towns were blown up on a regular basis. The corrupt judge was in league with the sheriff. Innocent men escaped the gallows; someone shot the rope. A lonely man has ridden into town. He is hot and dusty, but a galvanised tin bath will be provided for him and, as he is overpowered by soap-suds, some jumped-up punk will try to shoot him, unsuccessfully.

Then we cut to the scene on the honky-tonk floor where the fiddlers and the banjo-pickers are playing some old redneck breakdown and the guy gets to meet the probable girl who might be a school-marm and sings gospel songs with her own foot-pedalled harmonium accompaniment and likes black kids. As they swing each other on the dance-floor, their eyes meet for some misunderstood split second where they think they are in love – whatever love might be, as some distraction to the plot – and then they go back to their maladjusted places. For the guy will ride off into the sunset, as the harp or mouth-organ or harmonica or French fiddle sings its envoy or farewell in some threnody of lost aspiration, punctuated by a slap of the reins and the clicking diminuendo of a horse's hooves.

Meanwhile back at the ranch, we have entered the ornate circumstances of The Crown Liquor Saloon and are ensconced in the box where James Mason sat in *Odd Man Out*, or where he should have sat, had he not occupied a stage set. *Everything*, we argue with late adolescent passion, *is relative*, and we adduce quotations from J.W. Dunne's *An Experiment with Time* to back our case:

> 'From the windows of our railway carriage,' says Professor Eddington, 'we see a cow glide past at fifty miles an hour, and remark that the creature is enjoying a rest.'
>
> This is an illustration which pleases in more ways than one; and I regret having to interrupt the reader's contemplation thereof in order to direct his attention to a picture painted in less enticing colours. But we have to get on. We are still, then, seated in the same carriage; but this is now standing at a railway station. Looking from the windows on the side remote from the platform, we perceive another train at rest upon the rails. As we watch it a whistle blows, and we become aware that our train is beginning to pull out. Faster and faster it goes; the windows of the opposite train are running swiftly across the field of view . . . but a doubt arises . . . we miss the accustomed vibrations of our vehicle. We glance towards the platform windows, and discover, with something of a shock, that our carriage is still stationary. It is the other train which is moving.

In this mood of philosophical enquiry we leave The Crown. We negotiate gaslit shiny wet black sidestreets till we arrive at our Bohemia of Salisbury Street, this other annex of the universe which we had stumbled into some months before, led by a guru we had found in Bearnageeha.

The house was rented, I believe, by some minor faction of the Young Communist League, and I remember being briefly harangued by this chap in a red tie and National Health glasses; I countered with the classic Catholic apologetics taught to us by the Christian Brothers. The real politics, I think, lay in the music, and the ethos which lay behind the music: anyone could make music, and that music was for everyone, but you had to learn it, and you learned it from the masters.

So we sang in Ewan MacColl 'Scottish' or 'Cockney' accents and did more passable imitations of Bob Davenport's real Geordie, since our Belfast vowel sounds lay closer to it. Aspiring guitar-players were required to stagger their way through the intricate finger-picking of Bert Jansch's version of John Renbourne's 'Angie'. I bought *The Joan Baez Songbook* and learned the effete nylon-strung accompaniments. I fell in love with a girl with long black hair and a beautiful Spanish guitar. My love was not reciprocated, so I sang songs of unrequited love, and I believed in them.

I never owned a guitar, but I always borrowed. People shared. Packed into the two-rooms-knocked-into-one of Salisbury Street (as it was known), we felt ourselves to be in deep communion with confraternities and consororities across the world, as typified by Woody Guthrie's song version of *The Grapes of Wrath*, 'The Ballad of Tom Joad', or the shanty chorus of 'Go Down You Blood-red Roses'. We were in league with sailors, miners and whalers. And we drank our cider from its gallon flagon with our fingers crooked as we joined in on the Copper Brothers' Olde English cider-drinking song:

It was pleasant and delightful on a bright summer's morn
And the fields and the meadows were all covered in corn . . .

Indeed they were. Milkmaids under swaying yokes would wander into fields to be seduced. Jack Tars climbed the rigging. Highwaymen were heroes. There was an alarming incidence of incest. Young maids were advised of the handicaps of marrying old men. Hay was made and rolled in. Singing thrushes were ubiquitous on bushes. Reynard was 'Old Daddy Fox'. Broken tokens, Holland handkerchiefs and white cockades were badges of identity. Daughters had cruel fathers. There was blood in the kitchen and blood in the hall. Blacksmiths wielded their erotic hammers. Nurses were invariably false. One sister pushed the other sister into the mill-dam. Princesses lay down with gypsies. Joe Bloggs turns out to be the King of Spain. Girls had sexual intercourse with revenants. They enlisted in the army or the navy, dressed in men's array. Ploughboys whistled as they worked. Dogs had names like Dido, Bendigo and Traveller. Seven links were in a chain, and every link a year. And, as the song goes, 'like a bullock felled in Smithfield' was 'Napoleon Boney Part'.

Some of us in Salisbury Street – I remember John Moulden, Frankie Blaney, Sean and May McCann, Colette Woods, and me – invented ourselves into a 'folk group', unembarrassed by our title,

The Performers. Hovering between two stools – and stools were what folk singers perched on, when on stage – between description and prescription, this limp pseudonym expressed our *Weltanschauung*, which understood a text or rubric buried in some deep sleep, waiting for the kiss and imminent release of our performance. We were like a sacerdotal order, interceding on behalf of our interpretation of the *vox populi*, like a Russian Orthodoxy chanting invocations of the saints by smoky incense-light. We were Talmudic scholars, pondering the sacred meanings of the verb 'to perform': to do; to carry out duly; to act in fulfilment of; to carry into effect; to fulfil; to bring about; to render; to execute; to go through duly; to act; to play in due form; to do what is to be done; to execute a function; to act, behave; to act a part; to play or sing; to do feats, tricks, or other acts for exhibition . . . On our slightly-elevated platform, balancing upon our stools, we were mediators, as we occupied the space between the living and the dead, and sang in accents mangled by received LPs.

Some time around this time – a linear progression escapes me – we got into the Folk Music Club at Queen's University, which was held in the dank sepulchral basement premises of the Anatomy laboratory. On musty shelves, foetuses and *lusus naturae* shuddered in their glass vats as the room reverberated to a shanty chorus or the pounding foot accompaniment to someone's violent red accordion playing. For here, unlike Salisbury Street, Irish music had equal rights with English Folk Revival. Here were flutes and fiddles. Here were boys up from the country, from the far-flung sheughs of Tyrone and Fermanagh. Or at the very least, boys from Belfast who had heard the real thing, and learned jigs and reels and songs in accents all their own, or close approximations of them. Around this time, or something like it, The Performers reached the high point of their brief career, playing 'warm-up' to the English folk-singer Shirley Collins at the Belfast Festival at Queen's. In the high Victorian sub-gothic Great Hall, the carved rafters rang to songs about the pits and planks of dear old England.

Hold on. For, as I recall it now, I sang Paddy Tunney's version of 'The Rambling Boys of Pleasure', that song which is the better matrix of 'Down By the Sally Gardens' than Yeats' parlour treatment, and which I learned from an LP my sister Caitlín had got hold of. There must have been another conterminous dimension of the Irish stuff going on before I even entered the Anatomy Museum, for I'd sung this song for years and, as I write, in 1996, I sing it still. I learned the songs of Nioclás Tóibín and Joe Heaney and Seán Mac Donnchadh, who sang in obscure dialects of Irish, recorded on the long-defunct EP (extended play) format of *Gael-linn*. I sang them in the upstairs room in an entry off Lower Donegall Street opposite where Sam Murray's workshop is now (it was the Ulster Folk Society then); where I first heard Cathal McConnell playing a tune with two whistles at the same time (made possible, as I discovered long afterwards, by invisibly Sellotaping the top three holes of one whistle); where Robin Morton would sing in a fog-horn Ulster accent to dispel our English-folky notions; where I sang 'The Rambling Boys' with a cold, and John Moulden told me I was all the better for it – perhaps it corresponded to an Ulster honk. I sang '*Máirín de Barra*' and '*Casadh an tSúgáin*' and '*An Caisideach Bán*' and '*Eochaill*' and '*An Sceilpín Draighneach*'. I became exotic for my Irish-speaking.

And yet. I also sang 'McCafferty' *à la* Ewan MacColl, in an histrionic Cockney, and I'd heard it sung as a child by my Grandma in her Falls Road accent, but somehow didn't connect the two. I sang it with my own guitar accompaniment in Salisbury Street before its downfall or demise, which had been initiated by the long-since-defunct tabloid Belfast paper, *Cityweek*. Dutiful investigative reporters had abandoned their habitual gaberdines and slouch hats for duffel coats and woolly scarves, and had infiltrated the aforesaid premises. They had mingled freely with persons of both sexes, long before 'sex' would be replaced by 'gender'. They were offered cider at the door. They said, 'Cool'. The air was blue with dubious cigarette smoke. Girls appeared to have nothing on beneath their bum-length V-necked beatnik mohair sweaters. The outside lavatory was communal. In fact, the whole place was communal or free-thinking, and these reporters were astonished at the freedom which abounded on the premises and the opinions volunteered to them unasked. There was much promiscuous and uncalled-for singing. A so-called entertainer in a Pancho Villa moustache perched on a stool next to the Victorian fireplace and sang the words 'tea' and 'sugar' with a bluesy innuendo.

By now, the air was blue entirely: sapphire, turquoise, Cambridge-blue and Oxford-blue, hyacinth and bluebell-blue abounded on the premises of indigo and slate; various planes and dimensions were disturbed from Prussian regiments of azure and forget-me-nots, as the whole blue laminated archaeology was transformed by the smoke and gutturals of solitary singers into Lawrentian gentians of Pluto-blue. The duffelled-up reporters thought it just as well they'd worn dark glasses, for they did not want to be imbued with blue. And then they went upstairs into a further, bluer zone.

DOES YOUR CHILD GO TO THIS PLACE?
– A special *Cityweek* exposé –

the headlines proclaimed. I was eating a Saturday fry when the news broke. 'What was the name of that place,' said my mother, 'that you used to go and study folk-song in?' 'Oh,' I said, with some pretend aplomb, 'there's a lot of houses in Salisbury Street, they must have been somewhere else.' The matter was let drop.

Then, one Sunday afternoon, when John Moulden was conducting his folk soirée where we debutants of folk were playing our guitars and singing our socially-aware folk-songs in workshop fashion and we were undergoing *education*, for God's sake, and I was singing someone's version of 'East Virginia' with a borrowed guitar and I'd come to the line:

> All I want is your love darling,
> Won't you take me back again?

and there was a knock at the door and someone politely opened it. There stood my mother and my father in their Sunday coats, and my mother took one look at this Bohemia and cried, 'Sacred Mother of God, come you out of there, Ciaran!' I had no option but to go. I did my duty as a true performer. Shamed before my peers, I went reluctantly, and afterwards, for years, I used to hear the cry of peers, going, 'Sacred Mother of God, come you out of there, Ciaran!'

Salisbury Street closed down soon afterwards. Not that it was ever open, in the way the Boom-Boom Rooms or The Plaza or The Orpheus were open, where you paid to drink warm Coca-Cola and shuffle on a crowded sweaty floor to uniforms of dance-bands; and everybody went there. Salisbury Street was an insider's state of mind. And after its demise, the action moved elsewhere, to whatever places might accommodate that cast of mind. New roads opened up; peripatetically, we followed them, over many years.

Around the World for Sport

But there is community in despised professions
and when the street musicians look down
into the deep red or blue linings of their instruments' cases
they are like divers, like archaeologists
discovering for the first time after centuries of burial,
centuries of invention and vast migrations no one understands,
a lost beauty, a vanished art like a living face –
Philip of Macedon's tomb.

from 'Street Musicians' by John Ash

We used to play in pubs, houses, buses, cars and aeroplanes; we played on roadside verges, backs of lorries and street corners; in backyards, gardens, haystacks, alleyways and entries; in chip-shop doorways and in Chinese restaurants; we played in schools and old folks' homes and hospitals; we played for visiting ambassadors and Lord Mayors of small rural boroughs; we played in festivals and *feiseanna* and *fleadhanna*; in competitions miscellaneous and specific; we played for dancers and non-dancers; we played on boats on seas and loughs; we played for the lifeboatman in Orkney on his night-shift; we used to love to play in public toilets for their great acoustics; we played in the Falls Baths, Belfast, and in the Bonnie Doon Shopping Mall in Edmonton, Alberta; we played on motorway hard shoulders and abandoned railway platforms, on mountains and by mountain streams; we played for seals on the shore of Rathlin Island; we played on piers and promenades and broken bridges; we played in broken-down trains to pass the time; we played in markets, fairgrounds, and in grand piazzas; we played in bushes, hedges, ditches; we played in Garrison; we played for demonstrations and assertions of the world to come, for Civil Rights and Women's Lib; we competed with the discos next door in hostelries far and near, and couldn't hear ourselves; we played in Dockers' Clubs and Postmen's Clubs and Bakers' Clubs; we played for Polish and Brazilian seamen; we played beneath the stars and as the sun was rising; we played in vacant pigsties; we played in snowstorms under butchers' awnings, and in the long grass at the back of rural pubs in summer; in mountain shacks and shebeens and in Italian cafés; we played mutedly in 'shut' pubs on Good Friday and in the Holy Hour on Easter Sunday; in Floral Halls and Orange Halls; we played in The Arcadia; we played in The Felons' Club and in The Trocadero; we played in front of the Acropolis.

I cannot fix a linear chronology on these remembered tangled fragments. Itinerant, we have walked the same arbours many times, and have rephrased our questions and responses. Some grooves are worn deeper in our brains than others, as we go back to a favourite tune at staggered intervals; or, mental synapses are zapped, creating fractal pathways where we scarcely know the route, as when we hear a tune we used to play, played differently by someone else. Perhaps the person picked it up from us directly, many years ago; maybe it had gone through many hands, as it must have done before it reached our ears; and who knows where it starts or ends?

We are in Garrison on the Fermanagh-Leitrim border. It is a late summer's evening. A gang of us – flute-players Gerry O'Donnell, Gary Hastings and myself; fiddle-players Mick Hoy, Andy Dickson, Seamus Quinn and Deirdre Shannon; the concertina-player and singer Gabie McArdle; and others – have been recruited from the pub. The Festival committee have switched on the fairy lights that drape the back of the lorry parked in the carpark; the lough beside reflects a still-enduring streak of sky, and the whole dusk seems to glow. Precarious on the makeshift mobile stage, we play a few tunes to the crowd that's scattered round in knots and dots and couples. Then Gabie sings 'Edmund on Lough Erne Shore':

> Each step I take by the winding river
> Makes me reminded of days of yore . . .

The song ends; there is a little ripple of applause. Someone comes up and hands us cigarettes, and asks for 'The Harvest Home'. We sit and talk and smoke a while, then nick our cigarettes and start to play. Almost instantly, one knot of the crowd unravels and this old man in a topcoat and a hat and big boots tied with yellow laces steps out. From another dark annex of the carpark, his counterpart appears. By the time we hit the last part of the first part first time round, they're poised and ready – arms not stiff and rigid like the modern over-educated dancer, but relaxed, palms held outwards in a gesture some way between a welcome and a challenge. They face each other, one foot pointing outwards, while the crowd has shifted and coagulated round them in a focus of attention.

But they have space, the dancers. As we hit the first part of the repeat, their feet begin to move. Their hands accompany the dance in little wristy arcane movements, thumbs alternating with their digits. Their feet are hardly off the ground as they heel and toe and tap, till it seems there is a skim of twilight shimmering between their boot-soles and the black wet tarmac. Loose change jingles in their pockets as they waver gravely in the pre-determined figures, facing, backing off and circling, making pirouettes and formal quarter-bows, catching one another's little fingers on occasions, sometimes going for a full hand-clasp, instantly and rhythmically released. They *doppelgänger* one another. Nods and winks are witnessed as they undergo the subtle drama of the *ceili* house. They reinvent the past and all their past encounters; then the pattern comes to its conclusion. Four feet stand on *terra firma* for one instant, then they break apart and take the gait of normal human beings.

Everyone's relaxed, now. Cigarettes are passed around and lit. There is a surreptitious bottle full of who knows what. A buzz of conversation. Crack. Laughter shimmers out across Lough Melvin; the fairy lights are swaying, chinking gently in the desultory breeze . . .

Rubber Legs

But then I mind Keenan
and this man Brian McAleer,
there was a big barn dance in it one night
and the thing got going that good
and Brian came out of the kitchen.

Och, he was going on maybe seventy years of age at the time.
But a light, thin man, you know,
and always with good spirit.
Great singer too.
And him and Keenan hit the floor for a reel.
Well, if you seen them two men dancing, boy,
they were dancing from when they were young fellows, you know,
in their youth,
and still this was a great meeting for them
to meet again,
two old men, you know, they'd been dancing
whenever they were young fellows.
I'll tell you what they done too
and they sung together and they herded,
when there was no ditches and no fences about
and you went out and herded your cattle the whole day
and him and Brian was raised together.
That was Keenan's farm there
and McAleer's farm was here
and the two men herding on the one mountain together
and they sung together the whole day and exchanged songs.
And Brian and him going out that night on the floor
and if you seen them boys,
you would just think their legs was rubber.
I could mind Brian McAleer,
you want to see that man and him over eighty,
and the thin light legs of him,
and I can see him yet.
And Keenan was down below,
and Keenan was a small man,
a small tight wee man,
sort of wee pernickety man, you know,
and he was down there dancing.
And Keenan and McAleer was up
and then they would change places.
Well, you want to see McAleer;
you'd think the legs was rubber,
for a man like that, no pains nor arthritis nor rheumatism
nor damn what else.
He was quivering and carrying on with his feet

and Keenan was down below
and Keenan was putting in nice fancy steps, you know.
Ah Jesus, you want to see them two men dancing,
you could have played for them for a week.

John Loughran

... and now, we're in Trinity College in Dublin, some of the Garrison team, in this grandiose lecture theatre with tiered seats. There's bottles of stout at our feet and Gabie McArdle is singing 'The Banks of the Clyde'. His eyes have evaded the crowd and have fixed on the EXIT sign, and the song is one of those broken token numbers where the guy comes back after seven years and the girl doesn't get to recognise him till he whips off the false beard or whatever. And we're sitting with our hands propping up our chins, or holding a flute or fiddle in our contemplation.

As I roved out one bright summer's morning,
Down by the banks of a winding tide,
In ambush I lay where two lovers were talking
And clearly the streams they did gently glide ...

It is one of the peculiarities of this song that the hidden narrator disappears from view altogether after introducing himself in the first line. He is a mere witness, a device, an invisible function, a kind of *deus* in *machina*. And the poised artificiality of the encounter, its improbability, is mirrored by our circumstances, where we have crossed the subtle line between musician and entertainer, and we are on stage, sitting in our attitudes of histrionic relaxation. It is part of the musician's code of conduct to be deadpan, for this is not opera nor ballet. One does not interpret by bodily or facial countenance. The tune or song should speak for itself, though it is permitted for the audience to comment on the actions or rendition of a song. Verbal encouragement in the shape of a *sotto voce* 'Good man, Gabie' may be offered; but for our purposes, the real audience is not the one out there with their tiered gazing faces. The audience is us. Only we can offer what is deemed to be a proper response. I am wondering why this is so, or even if it is so, and it has something to do with the supposition that the ideal space for traditional music is a room.

This room is multi-functional. You can sit in it or stand in it or dance in it or eat and drink and talk in it. When a *ceili* is made, the dimensions of the room change subtly as the talk includes some news of the outside world. Music starts up, and the dimensions alter once again as dancers take the floor and those not dancing make space and squeeze up against each other, backs to the wall. 'Around the House and Mind the Dresser'. The room seems to expand or contract in Tardis-like defiance of the laws of time and space. Faced with the amphitheatre of a lecture hall, the musicians have to make their own room, or feign one.

Even in a so-called public house, dimensions are shaped by where the music-makers sit, and there is a socially-defined line between them and the punters or the drinkers or the talkers or the bookies' runners or the drug-dealers and all the other denizens of bars. Woe betide the naive yellow-anoraked German who takes a musician's seat, especially if the seat is obviously unoccupied, and has been for some time, and might still be before the night is out. The space was reserved, while the absent banjo-player had gone out on the rip and was last heard staggering through 'The Nine Points of Roguery' in the loo of The Liverpool Bar.

And everyone is supposed to know that these *are* the musicians' seats, so inevitably you get the situation where the session is supposed to start around nine, or half-past, or whatever, and the after-work drinkers are still ensconced after failing to make the third taxi they'd ordered, and the fiddlers and fluters are standing round in feigned nonchalance at the bar, and eventually the barman has to make some complex explanations about space and time, and orders them their final taxi. Gradually, the musicians filter down and take their empty seats in broken rhythm, and, yawning, put their instruments behind them as if they were some mere addenda to the main agenda. Then someone takes off his coat and piles it on top of the fiddle-case on the ledge at his back. More coats pile up, till somebody decides to make an archaeological investigation and exhume a flute-case. It's placed down on the table in between the pints and shorts and cigarette-packs. There is a lull or buzz of desultory talk before the catches are snapped open and the fluter gazes at the blue interior as if it was a pencil-or-a-gun-case or a geometry kit equipped with compasses, French curves, protractors and a double-sided rubber or eraser.

Then someone says, 'Are we going to play tunes or what?', and there is a sudden general upheaval as cases are discovered and broken open like they were some vintage of an obscure year of noble rot, and with grand deliberation we uncork one bottle just to sip and savour. Gerry McCartney has got out the banjo that he's playing after having abandoned the banjo-mandoline and he strikes up hell-for-leather into 'Last Night's Fun' and everyone joins in.

We only play the one tune, since we're only starting up. Everyone attempts to get in tune, because to be in tune is a mysterious dimension you can only enter when you *are* in tune, and that depends on what you play. You can't really tune to one note – usually an A – because you'll bend the A a certain way in this tune or the other, or the fluter blows it sharp because he's overreaching it in his excitement, and the fiddle-player has to compensate. Or the fiddle-player's little finger is too small to make the reach, and the fluter has to come down. I think that being in tune has got something to do with being in time, because when you hit the beat, and get into it, you somehow tune automatically. You arrive at some instinctual, right-side-of-the-brain agreement with the other players, and you're then 'in tune'.

And being in tune is a function of time. You are in tune with what goes on. It is a form of cool. It is the way the players become blue votaries of time, and intercede with it, and beat their time in slightly different times embedded in their pedal movements. One rocks off his heel on the off-beat; another taps the noiseless air one inch above the floor; another dances, almost, with two feet. Many very good players don't budge their feet at all and their bottom halves are rooted to the floor with the calm aplomb of Buddhas. They are moving to an inner pulse.

Time accelerates or contracts. We make a contract with it to pretend that it will never overcome us. The space of a song is what – how many minutes? – but seven years have gone by and we are still waiting for a resolution. The sailor has embarked on some exchange of phatic gifts, and things are moving now, when Mick Hoy produces a flat pack of Gallaher's Blues, opens them theatrically, gets up from his seat and starts to tender them to the line of musicians. He is oblivious of any audience beyond ourselves: handing round the cigarettes, he is in a room; or, this expansive gesture is a way of stretching time and space to make the room include the actual room, the lecture hall, and all imagined audiences. Tokens are exchanged – the torn halves of dollar bill, the pack of Wrigley's gum, the broken ring. These are ways of buying time and making known our identity within it.

We draw slowly on our meditative cigarettes – 'Quality Time' – and hear Gabie in his other world still gazing at the EXIT sign as he comes up with the long-foregone conclusion:

> And you and I true lovers will never be parted
> For I'll wed with my Jane on the banks of the Clyde.

He pauses for a split second. Nods his head. Refocuses his eyes. The audience applauds. He looks a bit bewildered, as if he had been lost for seven years in some Celtic Twilight Zone, and is only just back: this world was otherwise. Each time the song is sung, our notions of it change, and we are changed by it. The words are old. They have been worn into shape by many ears and mouths, and have been contemplated often. But every time is new because the time is new, and there is no time like now. Blue smoke revives the moving air.

Now Mick Hoy is rosining his bow. He rosins away till it falls like snow. Then he passes round the rosin, and the other fiddle-players take a ritual rub of it. They start to play. They hit the time just right, and everybody else joins in.

The Rub of Rosin

I heard them telling someone about a boy
and I suppose I don't know
whether it was Wellingtons that he was wearing,
or some sort of ould rubber boot or something.
He was playing at this fire in the country kitchen.
That time, ye'd be took down to the room,
a fiddler was made a wee bit special
than the rest, ye know.
And he was asked down, ye see, but . . .
Whatever way he rosined at his bow the whole night,
there was a shower of rosin about his feet,
like white snow with this big lump of rosin
away at this pony's tail that was in the bow.
He got up anyway
and he headed away for the kitchen, do you see,
and I suppose it was a right bit of a swanky place
and a wee bit different be other places,
and the room a wee bit of carpet
and he sat down at the table to take his bacon,
meat or whatever he was getting.
The music men would get it before the rest, special,
ye see. Maybe the rest would get it a wee bit rougher,
the music men would always get it a wee bit special.
And dammit anyway, whatever way
his ould rosin was sticking on his feet,
he went to move, do ye see, for to get away from the table
and the mat that he was on,
or bit of carpet or whatever the hell he was on,
it came along with him.

And he rose and he went out through the door
and he had this bit of carpet away after him
and away on up by the fire again,
it was stuck to the two Wellingtons or the two rubber shoes.
Away on up with him, do ye see, away up in by the fire.
They tell an awful story about it . . .
a wee while after he was playing away
and this started burning, hot by the red coals, ye see.
Nobody ever mentioned it to him,
that it was stuck to his feet . . .
He took it out of the room with him,
and was away on up by the fire
and he started to play,
ye know where his chair was again,
this started singeing and burning then
and it was stuck in the ashes . . .
But whether it happened or not . . .
I've never rosined that much
that I'd be stuck to the floor with rosin, anyway.

John Loughran

The Cat Melodeon

Wellington boots, or waterboots, as we called them then, have the effect of summoning up my childhood. I remember vividly the uncomfortableness of my knee-length school socks down-gyving and unshackling round my ankles, till they bunched their way beneath my instep arches; or the shiny rubber smell of new boots and their warm pristine cotton-white interior.

On a summer's day it was good to stand sockless in waterboots in a swift-moving shallow of the Blackstaff and feel the ice-cold water wobble and burgeon round your legs, till you had the firm illusion you stood in water without boots, a *frisson* made all the more pleasurable as the current came up to within an inch of the liquorice-strip lip: put one step wrong, and your boots were flooded with a devastating suddenness. Or, running stooped like an Indian scout behind the cover of a hedgerow, you'd plunge one boot into a sudden dungy cow-hoof-churned morass and find it stuck there like Excalibur. Abandoning your Indian identity, you had to extricate your leg and hop off for reinforcements. And on rare mornings, you'd step confidently out into a snowy strangeness, and feel the satisfactory crump as your ribbed sole bit into the three-inch thickness and left a ridgy imprint there, like Wenceslas: 'deep and crisp and even'. The day wore on and the snow got more and more compressed, till, as you skated homewards in the blue twilight, your boot-soles crossed the countless prints of others; the transcendental evening echoed with the far-off cries of snowball fights and slides.

Now I am aged five. I live in 100 Raglan Street. I open the door into the wall of the solid warmth of the room. Coal-brick murmurs its slow glow in the hearth. My father has just got up from his post-night-shift sleep and is sitting by the fireside. He's playing the melodeon. The bone buttons tick and click, the bass growls sporadically beneath the treble tremolo, and sometimes it seems that the sound of the melodeon occupies my childhood like a continuous loop. But this is a trick of time, in which half-remembered snatches of a melody can stand for vast scenarios of years. And because the tune's implanted in my brain, I think that what I hear now with my inward ear is what I heard back then; but I invent, or intervene – I put in the missing notes I didn't know back then, and can never know again not knowing them. And yet, the tune can never be perfected or complete: each time it is played is only a rehearsal for the next time, when it will open up under new management, or take 'another handling', as they say. Its simple structure is not rigid, and perhaps the less notes there are, the more you can invest in them.

I am thinking of 'The Rose of Arranmore' and 'Nearer My God To Thee', two favourite tunes of my father's: one a jaunty waltz-time love song, the other a beautiful melancholic dirge which is inextricably bound up with Belfast, since they say it was played as the *Titanic* foundered slowly off the icy coast of Newfoundland. These tunes were testimony to the two halves of my father's psyche; or perhaps, on second thoughts, they were two aspects of the same psyche.

My father, to tell the truth, was not the best melodeon-player in the world, but he was true to himself. He knew no jigs nor reels, and all he played were songs. Songs, ostensibly, are 'easy'; but to bear proper witness to them you must feel them, and my father did, with his whole body. As the bellows moved, his lungs and chest would heave, and his larynx kind of buzzed and hummed along with it. The music was him.

It reminds me of Rick Epping, the Californian melodeon-and-concertina-player who plays the mouth-organ at the same time as either concertina or melodeon, the mouth-organ clamped in one of those devices that look like an American football player's face-mask. His eyes are nearly popping out of his head as he sucks and blows and draws and pushes like some music-hall contortionist. And I remember Rick telling me, with his eyes nearly popping out of his head, how in a dream he had found the ideal instrument, which was himself. A Dr Frankenstein had implanted ivory buttons in his chest and gold reeds in his voice-box and put valves in his lungs to give him a continuous air-flow: 'It's Melodeonman,' they gasped, as he ripped open his shirt and exposed his buttons. Rick was also the epitome of the rhyme 'Skinnymalink melodeon legs, big banana feet / Went to the pictures and couldn't get a seat', which my father would utter in Pavlovian fashion any time he saw a long thin man. I think again of the integrity of his playing and how often I've tried to imitate his apparently random basses set against these simple little grace-notes – no, it's more the pulse, his feel for hitting or dwelling on a note, that I can never manage, since I am not him.

The melodeon, as a glorified mouth-organ, is the simplest of its vast extended family, known as 'free reed' instruments. The free reed is a metal tongue screwed or riveted over an accurately cut aperture in a metal frame and is caused to vibrate by air pressure supplied by mouth or bellows. As an accordion-tuner put it to me once, 'You see your reed, and the slot it goes in, they have to sit dead tight. There must be no daylight getting through. You'd be walking around inside that box, and if you could see daylight, well, that reed would not be set just right.'

These instruments come in ramifications of different shapes, sizes, systems and tunings, and are played as folk instruments throughout the world. In South America, the bandoneón (a kind of big square concertina) is the instrument *par excellence* to accompany the tango; Tex-Mex music would be unthinkable without the three-row diatonic button accordion; French café music uses a similar system, as well as the piano-accordion; in India, the hand-bellows-operated harmonium is used as an accompaniment to *ragas*; the driving beat of Louisiana Cajun music is based around the one-row melodeon, and so on.

In Ireland, various versions are played: chiefly, the two-row button accordion (or 'box'); the concertina; the piano-accordion; and the harmonica (also known as the French fiddle, the mouth-organ, or, in the USA, the harp), which has gained in popularity in recent years due to the great playing of the Murphy family from County Wexford. Things are complicated by the fact that these various free-reed instruments can be divided into two basically opposed categories: single action and double action.

Each system has its varying degrees of flexibility, articulation, ease or difficulty of fingering or bellows-work, and each has a significant impact on the structure of the music played. In double-action instruments, the depressing of a key or button will sound the same note on both the press and draw of the bellows: examples are the piano-accordion and the English concertina; but the Anglo-German concertina is single action, sounding two adjacent notes on the same button at the press or draw of the bellows. The one-row melodeon is single action, and so is the two-row accordion, which added another row a semi-tone down to make the instrument fully chromatic. In the opinion of many, single-action instruments, with their greater economy of fingering and the necessary articulation of the bellows, are more suitable for dance music.

The argument is further complicated by the fact that the two-row accordion has its own dichotomy, between instruments tuned B/C and those tuned C#/D, the former having less articulation. The late Joe Cooley played a C#/D box, and his style, with its rhythmic lingerings around the pulse, can be nicely contrasted with that of the maestro of the B/C system, Joe Burke, with his plethora of rolls and melodic variations. My brother-in-law, James McElheran of Cushendun, who played versions of the three-row box, the concertina and the two-row box before settling on the C#/D, remarked to me, in one of our episodic debates on the subject, how Joe Burke would 'make one of his wee detours round the fingerboard' – because it is sometimes difficult to play 'straight' on the B/C system – and come up with a wholly constructive variation. In other words, the system determines what you can do, and its limitations can inspire you.

Some systems, however, have more drawbacks than most, and the piano-accordion is in a class of its own. As the most fully-developed of the free-reed family, it is the least suitable for Irish dance music, though it is fair to say that some few brilliant musicians – James Keane and Leslie Craig, for example – have overcome its basic incongruity. However, there is no accounting for taste, and piano-box drivers abound, delighting in its multiplicity of basses, its inescapable relationship with the piano, its ability to fill a hall with noise, and its capacity, in some versions, to mimic a *ceili* band so that often, literally, they become one-man bands.

There are even admirers of the final abomination, the electronic piano-accordion, which is so big that the driver cannot carry it, but must sit it on a stand, and in its gadgetry, it is close to the karaoke machine; as is often the case, music is confused with technology. The piano-box misses one of the basic points of traditional music, that it should lie comfortably beneath your hands, and not outside your span; Paganini acrobatics are not what it's about. On the fiddle, you play in the first position, and your left hand doesn't move from where it's at; on wind instruments – whistle, flute, pipes – your hands can only be where they are, poised above the six or seven holes; your hands are handcuffed to the concertina by its straps; and even on the button-box, with its greater latitude, the notes are never that much out of reach. The length of the piano keyboard, however, determines that you nearly have to play with your arm, and to hold on to the fast time of a reel while hitting the right notes is difficult with an arm. Hence the tendency of many players to hit two simultaneous notes instead of one, a phenomenon known as 'playing between the cracks'. Thus the music is often reduced to a chromatic slabber.

The phrase 'cat melodeon' seems relevant in this context. In Ireland, it denotes a nadir of achievement or character, and can be applied to events, people, or performances. The 'cat' I believe comes from the Irish *cat marbh* or *cat mara* – literally, dead cat or sea cat – meaning a mischief or calamity. And piano-box players often jocularly refer to their instruments as 'melodeons'. It is not surprising that these two words have joined forces. As Ken Kesey says, 'You're either on the bus or off the bus'; and many cat melodeonists are off it.

Off the Bus

I have this *aide-mémoire* scrawled on the back of a bus ticket (it reminds me of the planned spontaneity of 'off-the-cuff' remarks, written up your sleeve like cog-notes) which says, 'Get into the bus via the box'. I think I know what it means: the box is a red Paolo Soprani two-row button accordion with its Fifties' bus-style radiator sound-grille and its bright pillar-box mock mother-of-pearl rounded edges like the top-deck shoulders of the omnibus as it swayed its vertical profile round curves and roundabouts. You could almost see some Finn McCool of an accordionist take up a bus and set it on its side on his gigantic lap and try to knock a tune out of it, as if its double row of windows at his right hand were accordion buttons, and the tune he plays is 'Smash the Windows'; the left-hand wheels are basses. The box of the bus reverberates.

I saw it yesterday, the old cross-town Gasworks-Waterworks double-decker, No. 77, resuscitated as a tourist venture of 'the peace process', antiquely teetering past the renovated Grand Opera House to make a right into Glengall Street and pause outside the HQ of the Ulster Unionist Party. For a moment I was back in 1965 or thereabouts, imagining the warm aroma of its leather seating and the conductor's ticket machine like a miniature horizontal melodeon. And the full-throated deep roar of its engine puts me in mind of how my father-in-law, the fiddler Paddy Shannon, would record the noise of the North-west 200 or the Ulster Grand Prix as motorbikes crescendoed and diminuendoed through the hedgy curves and braes of Country Antrim. Listening back to it, he'd know the rider by his sound-contour, which straight or hairpin he was about to take, and he could recall the weather by the hum or swish of tyres.

The whole terrain was mapped out on reel-to-reel recordings

that bike-and-music cronies knew by decibels and engine-tunings. Gathered in a kitchen or a front room, they'd listen to the race unfolding past their aural standpoint with its throttled troughs and highs of bass and treble. Appropriately wise-after-the-event remarks were made between rapt attentive silent taps of cigarette ash. After the race they would exhume their fiddles and their boxes from their boxes and strike up some apposite tune: 'Come West Along the Road', say, or 'The Long Chase', or 'Coming from the Races'. Their knees would scrape imaginary tarmac as they turned into the mind-bending bend or high part of the reel. They'd renegotiate the sound-track of the track.

Bikes and music go together, so Joe Cooley used to travel with his accordion strapped to the buzzing petrol-tank of the bike, on his way from one *ceili* to another via the rainy dirt-and-limestone roads of Connemara. And the noise of bikes reminds me of how the flute-player Gerry O'Donnell used to assert that the names of motor-cars bespoke their attributes: 'Rover', for example, was a long low growl, while 'Mini' was a verbal blip; when he pronounced the word 'bus', its abrupt labial accelerated into an elongated intermediary vowel, before ending with the sibilant 's' of brakes applied at bus-stops. 'Ford' rhymed with roared. 'Morris Oxford' and 'Austin Cambridge' were recited in their proper RP accents.

It occurs to me *en route* how many names for the various configurations of antique wheeled vehicles are derived from place names: 'coach' itself is from Kocs in Hungary; 'berlin'; 'landau'; 'surrey'; and *fiacre*, from the Hôtel de St Fiacre in Paris, which is in turn from the Irish *fiachra*, meaning raven-like. Then there are the other personal names: 'tilbury', not the docks in London, but the name of its inventor; 'clarence'; 'victoria'; 'hansom', from Joseph A. Hansom (1803–82); and 'brougham', from Henry Peter, Lord Brougham (1778–1868). 'Hackney' has an interestingly tangled etymology, since it would appear that the place was named after the beast, 'an ambling mare', from Old French *haquenée* (further history unknown, says *Chambers*); the *OED* mentions Skeat's view that 'horses were raised on the pasture-land there and taken to Smithfield through Mare Street'. It's a kind of horse before the cart idea.

It resembles, in its garbledness, the way we used to call Derrygonnelly in County Fermanagh Gerrydonnelly, after Gerry O'Donnell, the aforementioned flute-player, who used to rent a house or cabin outside of Derrygonnelly, in the townland of Derryvary (or Verydarry, as we'd say). After playing in The Cosy Bar into the after-hours, we'd walk the mile or so until we came to the white concrete winding laneway that in moonlight looked like The Yellow Brick Road in *The Wizard of Oz*, that led us to a farmyard, and then we'd stroll out across the pathless field, negotiating cow-pats and thistle-clumps, till we arrived at Verydarry. Devoid of trees, it was no longer 'Derry' meaning 'oak-grove', though Gerry, being an art student at the time, had found a huge piece of timber and had parked it in the front yard, undecided whether he should sculpt it or leave it as an *objet trouvé*, witness to the vanished grove. And 'grove', I learn from *Chambers*, is also 'a lodge of a benefit society called Druids'. Coincidentally, around this time, Gerry played in a band called *Na Draíodóirí*, or The Druids, or Wizards.

We were all apprentice Druids then, I think, led by the resident genius of Mick Hoy the fiddle-player. Stuck out in the starving wilderness, deprived of supermarkets, we'd improvise *cuisine* from sorrel, chickweed, nettles, mushrooms and wild garlic, inspired by the arcane herbal forage-knowledge of Gary Hastings. Soup was made in a vast antique cast-iron stockpot, and in the morning you would find the aluminium ladle standing vertically in a green glue residue.

Time got out of mind as last night's fun embraced the next hungover morning and we staggered out again into the dawn or afternoon to hunt for wild herbs. We were oxymorons, children of the Sixties caught in a Celtic time warp where tunes were handed on by fairies or acquired in dreams: dimly sceptical of magic, we found ourselves surrounded by it, and the old tunes we learned from Mick became our conversation. Even new tunes, like 'The Floating Crowbar' (I have heard it attributed to the fiddle-player Brendan McGlinchey), corresponded to a neo-Druidic sympathetic magic, where – so the story goes – the forged-steel murder weapon ditched in the river floated to the surface with the blood and hair of its victim still clotted to it. The reel took on the antique connotation of a Grimm's tale, with its talking horse's head that revealed the nub of the story in a cryptic rhyme. Mick would tell us tall tales:

> *There was this man*
> *used to be delivering Guinness, d'you know,*
> *the barrels of Guinness*

with a horse and a van
round the town there.

And it was a fierce hot day.
So, beGod, he went into this pub, anyway,
and he had a drink.
And when he came out again, beGod,
one of the barrels had bursted
with the heat of the sun, you know,
and it started flowing down
and the horse began to drink it, and beGod,
the horse got drunk, and he fell too.

So when the boy came out
the horse was lying
and he thought that he was dead,
and he prepared to skin him.

So he skinned him anyway,
and when he had him skinned
the horse got up again.
So he started off
and went and cut some rods,
some sally rods,
and he started scolloping the skin back on him.
So the rods started to grow on the horse.

And the next year, beGod,
they cut as many rods off the horse
as thatched six or seven houses!

'Scollop', here, is from the Irish *scailp*, a thatching pin, which might be cognate with Ulster English 'skelf', the tiny hypodermic splinter of wood you get embedded in your fingertip, if not with a sudden freezing 'skiff' of April rain. These jabs or shocks put me in mind of Allen Ginsberg's brilliant line, from a poem, 'Graphic Winces', which is a catalogue of such encounters:

> or at icebox grabbing the half-eaten Nestlé's Crunch
> a sliver of foil sparks on your back molar's filling.

This reminds me of the blue electric flashes in a dodgem arena where the trolleys judder on their ceiling-high of chicken-wire connections. Once, having escaped Verydarry, we encountered a small peripatetic fairground in a one-horse County Leitrim town, and did the dodgems, our rubber bumpers bouncing off each other's. So the music used to bounce from player to player, and we'd extend our index fingers to another's so as we would get the buzz, the subtle bolt of electricity that sparks between the near-contingent indices of God and Adam on the Sistine Chapel ceiling. Trying to visualise the painting's plaster-cracks, I'd find myself lying gazing at the bumpy crazy ceiling of the Verydarry bedroom, momentarily awake before I shut my eyes against the birdsong-torn dawn. Still, drunken patches of ambiguous damp that might be physiognomies or maps swam inside my eyelids; flecks and torn threads of matter drifted off into the unseen corners of my brain.

Such edgy peripheral vision has something to do with how Mick Hoy found a 78 in a blackthorn hedge, that had a pie-slice broken out of it, and anyway, he played it, and patched the shard into the tune by ear, and plays it to this day. It's probably apocryphal, like the story of guys in Harlem in the Twenties, playing black blues in jive joints. They couldn't afford the steel needles, so they got this dude with a fastidiously long-grown index fingernail which acted as a stylus stuck into the groove: precursor, maybe, of the 'scratch' DJ, whose anti-clockwise rhythmic spasms twist and turn the disc against itself, and a new broken beat emerges.

Mick was also reputed to have found a lump of rosin up a tree, when he was stuck for some: not the natural stuff that might exude from a pine, but the shop-bought variety that comes wrapped up in its yellow-duster cloth. How it got there is anybody's guess, but poteen or the fairies might have been involved. I don't know if the fiddle-player John Loughran spent much time in this neck of the woods, but he knew about such strange encounters:

> *The whole thing got going good, boy,*
> *and Nugent and McCabe playing for hell.*
> *Drinking poteen from . . .*
> *them big mugs and oul' things,*
> *might be a hundred years of age,*
> *some flowers on them.*
> *Them oul' mugs, y'know, blue bars around them,*

blue and white bars,
and that'd be all set around the petrol drum,
and them playing away and then
this two pound tin of Tate and Lyle
would come out and a big lion on the box
and his two paws out
and him looking round him,
this big bear or whatever he was,
like a big Alsatian
and the box would be left out
and everybody would go for this syrup
and you wouldn't have time to twist it up
or screw it up, ye know,
and ye'd have your farl of bread in your hand
and do all the thing yourself
after the table was set
and you'd put the lid up on the syrup
and ye start to twist this knife around
or spoon, to try to get it out.
And some boy going away by the fire
away by his chair or wherever he was
and this string o' syrup away out after him,
away on, and that was all in good favour
and was grand.

You come out of Nugent's
at three, two o'clock in the morning
and there was talk of ghosts being about.
Damn, the hell you cared whether you seen a ghost or not.
And anyway, there was Nugent
this one night
and this poteen was going about
and Nugent,
somebody thought he was going to destroy the bow
and somebody went over,
put their hand over,
and took the bow out of his hand,
and Nugent fiddled away with no bow,
away on, up and down
and they thought that maybe he'd get very bad

and that he'd drop the fiddle
and somebody just went over
and catched the neck of the fiddle.

He played away the night
with no fiddle up here
and he played away with no bow down below.
The poteen was in and working well, boys,
while he played away at these tunes.
That's what Nugent would do, ye see . . .
Nugent was a terrific player
and wouldn't play
if he thought he was making mistakes
or letting himself down,
he wouldn't play at all
if there was too much drink on the job.
But the poteen now was going good, ye see.

And after that he was coming home with the fiddle
by this oul' ruin of a house –
he told me himself –
ah, he probably seen a light
or he thought there was a light in it
and he staggered into it.
The house was down, I think, bravely scattered maybe,
there'd been nobody in it for years.
He thought he was in a wake house
or something,
to hear him tell it, or some damn thing,
there'd be all this crack about it . . .

Ay, he thought there was a crowd.
But maybe it was just where he left,
maybe he was playing the fiddle
the while before,
it was still in his head the whole time maybe.
Oh, he played all right for the dancers,
he could mind going into it and all.
But there was no place there.
Sure the house was down at the time.

Oh, good stuff that poteen . . .
Ye'd never be alone.
A crowd of ye if ye took plenty of poteen.
Ye'd see plenty round ye.
Ay, surely to God, oh aye,
they'd multiply
and where there'd be one
when ye left there'd be twenty-one.
Oh, poteen was the quare stuff . . .
But when you could play away
and the bow not there at all, it was good.

So, imaginary music was inclined to hover in the cracks of Verydarry dawns and filter through our brainpans as if there were a troupe of fairies hidden in the bushes outside, playing tiny pipes and whistles backwards like a garbled tape-recording or the dim cacophony of a remembered *fleadh* as you approached the town and overheard its music miles away, swelling and fading, wafting on the desultory breeze. On the verge of sleep, our memory banks would leak out bits and sound-bites, and the cock would crow an hour ago in that split second where we'd reeled from one tune into the other, and his five raucous haiku syllables made a counterpointed intervention with the rhythm of the first bar. In between the underlying chinks, we'd hear the crazy aural map of newly-awakened birds and sheep, a buzz of conversation or a paradisal queuing at the tympanic entrance to the ear, about to be received into its labyrinth.

From time to time we would make lethargic attempts to leave Verydarry and would go down to the heat-shimmered minor road and watch it ooze and melt. The heavy air was redolent with tar and fuchsia blossom. Blackbirds whistled variations on the first bar of an uncollected reel. Drugged by July and crazy music, Deirdre and I would stand there like two petrol pumps for hours. An occasional car droned by, going elsewhere. A tractor passed us and left thick wavy chevrons printed on the road. Time passed . . . eventually we would return to the house. We would fill the earthenware sink with cold spring water and plunge our hands up to the wrists in it to feel the bracelet-cool about them.

The stone walls and flags contained a block of damp micro-climate, and if walls could talk, their message would be garbled.

For, as the molecules of the stone are altered slightly by the timpani of music and received discussion, it becomes a kind of lithophone. A tuning fork struck against it will resound with buzzes of a thousand sessions overlayered and embedded there in various degrees of promiscuity. 'The Floating Crowbar' floats above 'The Maid behind the Bar', beneath 'The Blackthorn Stick', and it is difficult to extricate a phrase from a competing other. Seekers of ghosts have recorded conversations in haunted empty rooms, and the house in Verydarry had a shiver of dark atmosphere.

We were advised by Gary that in order to escape we would have to put our jackets on back-to-front and inside-out, this being a well-known antidote to spells. The Wren Boys on their annual Stephen's Day foray would do the same, thus rendering them anonymous. And in order to escape the world you temporarily inhabit, you must take its guise, put your arms into its reversed sleeves and pull them out of themselves to show their blue pin-striped linings. You must walk backwards into the future like a Frankenstein monster with extended sleepwalker's arms.

Inside-out or not, a neighbour's neighbour finally gave us a lift to Enniskillen and, with one bound, we were free. There and then, we took the bus to Sligo on our route to the far West.

Marking Time

The year is 198—, and we, by dint of polyphonic after-hours negotiation, by hooks and crooks of bendy roads and out-of-kilter crosses, past the two immobilised Shell petrol pumps stationed on the mossy forecourt of a disused garage, have arrived at O'Looney's Bar, somewhere in the hinterland of Miltown Malbay. It is hardly recognisable as a building, let alone a bar, from its ivy-overgrown outside: it looks more like a hedge – if 'hedge' means 'to shuffle, be evasive, as in argument' – for O'Looney's status as a bar is open to debate. It is, more likely, 'a public house', in its archaic connotation as 'a house open to the public', where the consumption of alcohol is, ostensibly, an afterthought. Or it is a 'shebeen', from the Irish *séibín*, 'a little mug', diminutive of *séibe*, 'a hole, an orifice; a liquid measure, a mug, a bottle' – Dinneen cites the interesting *i mbéal na séibe*, literally, 'in the mouth of the séibe', i.e. 'suddenly', or 'unexpectedly', which seems appropriate to O'Looney's. It is impossible to find the front door in its branchy leafy frame of reference, so we go round the back, which is, after all, the customary mode of entry at this unconstitutional hour of the night or morning. In O'Looney's, buried in illicit time, for time out of mind, the front door has become defunct, embedded like a Sanskrit fossil in the Irish-English tongue, its creaking hinge of language rusted stiff for ever.

We knock. We knock again. The back door opens up to this ambiguous gloom we walk into. The floor is earth. The smell is mould and alcohol and earth and smoke of turf and nicotine. Candles gutter in their yellow cataracts of wax. A turf fire glows at one end of the room. There is a makeshift bar at the other. In between are shapes hunched over instruments and tunes and tables. Feet pound the earth floor. I get these bearings gradually, as we have some stumbling time to seat ourselves after taking stock of the bar with its basic choice of bottles: stout and whiskey. I find myself wedged in a three-foot-deep window-ledge. Gazing upwards through the rafters as the music becomes a mantra, I scan some isolated stars through the holes in the thatch. It could be 18—, but the Guinness calendar affirms that it is otherwise: it is April 1953. 'You can do what toucan do', the slogan says; 'slogan', from the Irish or Gaelic *sluagh-ghairm*, a battle-cry, or, more accurately, the 'outcry of a crowd'.

And like some antiquated battle-cry of here and now, the Cooleas start up. The Cooleas are up for the weekend from Cúil Aodha, this tiny Gaeltacht on the Cork and Kerry border, and in Coolea, songs are currency. They sing big *sean-nós* songs. They sing comic songs and songs of repartee. They sing newly-made songs on the coming of electricity to Coolea, or the first clock ever brought there, and the same clock was kicked useless for its not keeping time, whatever 'time' was back then. They stand their ground in a polyphonic circle in the middle of the floor, holding hands and shoulders as the grain of each voice vibrates against the others and illuminates the others, and their thrown shadows grow enormous on the bumpy pockmarked whitewashed wall and mingle with our shadows. The candles sway and loom, the earthen floor goes 'om', the whole room pulses like a bellows, and the turf fire flares up suddenly to throw the rapt attentive faces of the listeners into chiaroscuro.

They are not an audience, for 'audience' implies a passive formality, and most of these listeners will do something before the night is out: they will sing themselves, or play or dance or tell a yarn or 'recimitation', or keep time to the music by a rhythmic rattle of the loose change in their trouser-pockets. Some non-musicians will have the knack of knowing tunes through and through – perfect listeners, for whom it is a joy to play – and, as founts of polyonymous nomenclature, will be ready to supply a name, or several, to the tune known to its player as 'the one after the one that goes before it'. Or some guitar-player, oblivious to protocol, after footering and tuning, will start up a three-chord accompaniment in the wrong key in the middle of someone's unaccompanied song. Someone else will comment on the player's marvellous 'accomplishment'.

This is not an audience, but a gathering which invents its programme as it goes along, navigating through the night by dint of many pilots. And the lulls are purposeful, asterisks in time which point eight different ways, like the eight bars of a reel with all its variations. Contracts are made within these temporal nodes; the room becomes an internet. Through the portal of O'Looney's we glimpse the starry fragments of a great galactic internet which shimmers over all the shebeens of the earth – in Ballyvourney or in Boston, in Sydney or in Springfield, Massachusetts, wherever gatherings like this take place and make their sidereal observations. Across the many time zones the same tune might be bi-located at the same time, in the same time.

Layers of cigarette smoke, blue as a Gitanes or Disque Bleu packet, vacillate through the room like microcosmic wavebands. Their frequencies are sputtering and crackling as they're assailed by atmospheric interference and black noise leaks out from the cracks between the lighted station blips. The musicians are like double agents, flitting through the complicated frontiers. They ride the Disque Bleu logo with its wings of Mercury through the Logos of the blue smoke internet and all its shifting laminates. They are subversives of a kind, and they withstand the efforts of officialdom. They will not be regimented, for they are a Maquis, the Second World War Résistance or guerrilla force; *maquis*, from the thicket formation of shrubs on Mediterranean shores, that I imagine is a smoky blue like lavender, shimmering across the scrubby landscape bordering the Raoul Dufy sea. They are not easily uprooted, for their roots are deeply intertangled and form complicated family trees of mutual support. Confederate or Union agents, they blend invisibly across each other's lines, till their blues and greys meet in some other aspect of the spectrum, and another shade of ambiguity is formed. They take each other's versions on and learn each other's shibboleths; 'shibboleth' from the Hebrew for 'torrent':

> Then Jephthah gathered together all the men of Gilead, and fought with Ephraim: and the men of Gilead smote Ephraim, because they said, Ye Gileadites are fugitives of Ephraim among the Ephraimites, and among the Manassites.
>
> And the Gileadites took the passages of Jordan before the Ephraimites: and it was so, that when those Ephraimites which were escaped said, Let me go over; that the men of Gilead said unto him, Art thou an Ephraimite? If he said, Nay;
>
> Then said they unto him, Say now Shibboleth: and he said Sibboleth: for he could not frame to pronounce it right. Then

they took him and slew him at the passages of Jordan: and there fell at that time of the Ephraimites forty and two thousand.

Judges XII, 4–6

Musicians learn to get their tongues round things. They are chameleons, and have independent eyes by which they recognise each other while they blink at someone else. They understand that time itself is a chameleon, so they mark it and they keep it, and they syncopate it. Creatures of a changing blue lagoon, they drift down through its depths like shoals of semiquavers, making new tunes as they swim in temporal agreement.

By this time, dawn is tumultuous in O'Looney's, one singer raising his voice against the chorus of progressively-waking birds; the window slowly transforms indigo to sapphire. Then we stumble out into a vast sky opening up before us in a panoply of pink and blue and gold and purple flocks, the bleating of innumerable sheep.

O'Looney's is one of those subjunctive venues where musicianers evade the *hoi polloi* of the designated festival or *fleadh* town. Established by anecdote and shibboleth, they are arrived at by elaborate routines; false trails are laid and misdirections given out. In the town itself, there is a complex ranking of the various pubs, according to their suitability for music and their owners' sense of protocol. Once an equilibrium of musicianers and public is established, the wise owner locks his doors to all those who have not been hitherto initiated. The foolish owner's eyes light up with dollar signs: accessible to all and sundry, his bar is inundated and the music swamped; his returns diminish rapidly, as the music goes elsewhere.

Finding the right bar is a game of chance and skill suitable for x amount of players, and the rules are phrased in a future conditional tense. Clever punters (members of the listening public) will stake out salient pubs and observe the ratio of instrument cases being carried in, then make their move. A cohort of runners will impart the information to the other members of this pact of punters. Meanwhile, musicians leave false scents, like wearing L'Air du Temps instead of Brut; there is an undercover *noir* to everything, as everyone is shadowed. Demographic shifts are made, as many people throng and filter through each other in the street in search of nodes and modes of entertainment and the crack. Paths cross many times and the whole town is a layered chart of footprints.

You cruise the town until the cruise becomes a trawl and possibilities are narrowed down: it's like eating out in London's Soho, where you peruse the menus of a hundred eating-houses and it's pot luck whether you eat well or not. You pass the same enticing restaurant so many times that you eventually succumb to its temptation; or, completely spoiled for choice, you are gastronomically confused, and end up with the wrong choice. There are no guarantees, for even the best of places have their off-nights. Trying to allow for all the possibilities, you will be circumvented by the circumstances. So, while there might be some general agreement as to the quality of a *fleadh*, there might be general confusion: one person's *fleadh* is not another's, and not everyone can be in the right place at the right time.

As the town is saturated, movement becomes difficult. It is not unknown for a rake of musicians to play, drink, eat, talk and sleep in the same establishment for four days; and knowing when to stay put requires some art or wisdom. You have to know how to make the best of what there is, and settle for it; and the supposition of a better time elsewhere is mere illusion. Getting there, you have to tune in to the different frequencies of time as your antennae pick up sonic blips and bleeps and the static comes through like the gargled blue noise of locomotive whistles. There are dialects of moods, décors, atmospheres and ambiances. You can fall through trapdoors.

Some unscrupulous publicans, for instance, will put out the word that they have opened up this well-appointed backroom or annex which will extend well after hours, and lure the music in with promises of hospitality. Then when you arrive, you find you are transformed into performing monkeys. There is a cover charge for eager tourists, and there is no escape for you because it's after hours. You are effectively imprisoned: if 'animalcatraz' is US slang for 'zoo', then this place is a 'ceolcatraz'.

Or you find the ideal quiet pub with gorgeous wooden floors and fixtures mirrored in its antique trade mirrors, and you imbibe its atmosphere until you realise that the eccentric owner has forbidden music. He wants his usual clientèle and schedule – 'schedule', from the Latin diminutive of *scheda*, 'a strip of papyrus', something like a bar tab or a check-out print-out with its serried hieroglyphs and computations, marking time and money. He does not want to have his everyday disturbed. He values normal custom. His venue is a discreet forum for the savouring of modicums of talk and alcohol.

Jorums are poured as conversations hush around them. A cigarette is lit; a tiny hiss. Ash falls to the quiet floor. And you leave feeling some respect, because there always should be room for this; you realise your status as an interloper.

By this time all the other bars you sussed out hours ago have been packed, so you end up playing in the disused bus station where dogs scavenge for left-overs in the greasy drift of discarded fish and chip and sausage wrappings. Someone has procured a Judas (from 'Iscariot' – 's carry-out) and it's passed around while two drunks shape up for a fight, take a swing at one another and fall down to snore beside each other.

Similarly, you get to know the various dimensions of window-ledges round the town, where three or four musicianers can wedge themselves and set up an impromptu session. Punters gather in a semi-circle, till from the street the players are invisible; and in this respect, I remember how old punters would perch their antiquated ghetto-blasters on a window-ledge and give the crowd the benefit of their prized recordings of the fiddle competition. From beyond the semi-circle, it looks just like a session, to the extent that I once observed an ethnomusicologist holding her Nagra mike above the appreciatively nodding heads, the ears cocked to one side, while she footered with her levels and her headphones.

It's possible that such a tape of a tape resides, once or twice removed, in the hermetic archive of the Ulster Folk and Transport Museum. Not for the first time, I wonder about the coupling of 'folk' and 'transport', and am reminded that here, 'folk' is mostly 'material culture' – cottages, a spade mill, stone walls, a schoolhouse, handlooms, churches, and a water-mill. Of particular interest is a bleach-green look-out post built like a birdwatcher's granite sangar, from which the unseen sentry could observe the linen-rustlers, then step out and boldly sound the early-warning system of his pawl-and-ratchet, whirligig-type rattle. It reminds us that Ulster culture resides more in what you do than what you say or sing or play: O linen-weavers, builders of barns, rope-winders, intricate masons! It is but a short step to the vehicle: O makers of motor-bikes and tractors! Builders of the *Belfast* and *Titanic*! Constructors of the Harlandic diesel electric locomotive commissioned by the Buenos Aires Great Southern Railway Company! Perfectors of the four-cylinder, triple-expansion, steam-reciprocating engine!

And as children, we were proudly told that Belfast had the

biggest shipyard, rope-walk, linen mill, tobacco-works and match manufactory in the world. Even then, the 'had' was *passé*, but the myth persisted and I felt proud as well – Irish as I was, or am – to be a member of this Empire with its cornucopia full of works and pomps. Then, my father would take us to the old Transport Museum in Witham Street, before the concept 'folk' had been invented. This was a cold dank converted engine-shed or tram-depot. We loved its gloom and smell of oil and iron, the palpable whiff of steam long since expired. Enormous locomotives loomed above us as we gawped at them open-jawed. We would climb aboard a tram and sit in the open-top deck, and my father would sniff and wipe his eyes because he'd remembered his father taking him on board a tram just like this, and he could feel the wind of time blow in his ears and eyes.

The old Transport Museum persisted a good many years after the establishment of the Ulster Folk and Transport Museum at Cultra*, and I used to bring my own children there and experience that generational shiver. Now, the whole shebang has been transported, lock, stock and barrel, to Cultra, and housed in a giant glass and concrete hangar. The same enormous locomotives are there, somewhat diminished by the Brobdingnagian ceiling; and the atmosphere is different, for now everything is in a context. Many details have been added to convince us that the past is here and now. There is an authentic newsvendor's kiosk; pockmarked enamel adverts for defunct brands of tea and cigarettes; the café is a station replica; period-costumed dummies relax stiffly in their leather-perfumed carriages. In one such thematic figment, a cassette of atmospheric platform noise is broadcast throughout the vast resounding hall: 'All ab-o-o-a-r-rd for Ballymena! Pe-e-e-p, pe-e-p! Whis-s-st. Psssst. Psst. Pst. Po-o-o-o-p, po-o-o-p! Choo-chuh-chuh, choo-chuh, chunk, chuff, chuff chuff. Ticka-tick-a-tick,' till it fades away and leaves behind imaginary puffs of smoke, and a lull of silence as the tape rewinds.

* Philologically, the Museum is aptly located. A straightforward translation of *cúl trá* might be 'behind the strand' or 'the hinterland of the strand' (cf. Scottish *ahint*, 'behind'); but *trá* as a verb means 'to ebb', and is surely related to *tráth*, 'a period of time; once upon a time; a season' and other time-related concepts. So the place name might be glossed as 'the hinterland of time', or, 'at the back of once upon a time'. *Idir-thráth* is 'twilight'; so we are getting very close to 'the twilight zone'.

And they have added strange contraptions from the age of narrow-gauge: hybrid locomotive buses; tandem quadricycles; squat black Guinness mules that transported porter through the labyrinthine brewery; mobile donkey-engines from the shipyard; things that look like time-machines in their perfect, cast-iron, antiquated futuristic design, with their milled-brass knobs and thumbscrews, their plate-glassed Captain Nemo dials with steel needles stilled in them.

Everything is analogue, and looks like something else. Everything is *déjà vu*.

The Dead Man's Breeches

No one on first seeing the machine could possibly imagine its object. It has a heavy cast-iron base, or bed-plate, about fifteen inches long and six wide, and perhaps one inch high. At each end is an upright standard of steel, three inches long, and on these two standards is supported a steel spindle about thirty inches long. A flue-screw thread is cut on this, and by means of other screw threads in the holes at the top of the standards, the spindle can be made to move to the right or left on turning the handle at the end of the spindle.

The handle is at the right, and at the other end is a heavy balance-wheel, to give steadiness to the motion. The spindle is thus a horizontal screw, that may be screwed backward or forward for nearly its whole length. In the centre of this screw is a brass cylinder, about nine inches long and three inches thick. This is firmly fastened to the spindle, and moves with it whenever the handle is turned. On this cylinder is cut a very fine spiral groove, about one-tenth of an inch deep, and extending over the whole cylinder in a continuous groove from end to end.

At the side of this cylinder is a mouthpiece, and behind this, supported by a brass framework, is an iron diaphragm, the two parts being precisely like the mouthpiece and diaphragm of a telephone. Behind the diaphragm is a delicate metal point or stylus, supported by a tiny brass spring, and joined to the diaphragm by a small ring of rubber, fastened on with sealing-wax. The mouthpiece, diaphragm and stylus are supported by a bracket that rests on a swinging arm secured to the base of the instrument.

This is all that appeared as I sat down to the table beside the machine while my friend, the professor, prepared to show me how and why it worked. He took up a long smooth sheet of tinfoil and wrapped it round the brass cylinder, and pasted it down with a little shellac. He then moved the arm that supported the mouthpiece, and pushed it close to the cylinder.

Charles Barnard, *The Youth's Companion*, 1878

I told some of you last Thursday of the principles of the Time Machine, and showed you the actual thing itself, incomplete in the workshop. There it is now, a little travel-worn, truly; and one of the ivory bars is cracked, and a brass rail bent; but the rest of it's sound enough. I expected to finish it on Friday; but on Friday, when the putting together was nearly done, I found that one of the nickel bars was exactly one inch too short, and this I had to get remade; so that the thing was not complete until this morning. It was at ten o'clock that the first of all Time Machines began its career. I gave it a last tap, tried all the screws again, put one more drop of oil on the quartz rod, and sat myself in the saddle.

H.G. Wells, *The Time Machine*, 1896

'Now', said he, 'you observe that the little stylus at the back of the diaphragm presses on the foil wrapped round the cylinder. If I now turn the handle of the spindle, the stylus will push the foil into the spiral groove, and make a continuous grooved mark on the foil'.

This he did, and I watched the machine as it turned and traced the fine indented mark on the soft foil. Then the professor stooped over the instrument and placing his lips near the mouthpiece, said, in a loud voice, 'Mr Charles Barnard has come to see the phonograph. Ha, ha! I do de-c-la-r-e!'.

It was rather queer to have one's name shouted out in this manner in the quiet laboratory, and I did not know what to make of the proceeding. A number of the students, hearing the words shouted out in this style, came near to see what was going on. Some of them laughed, as if they knew what was coming; but they said nothing, and stood waiting to see what would happen next. Then the professor drew back the swinging arm so as to remove the stylus from the foil, and then quickly turned the handle the opposite way. In a moment the screw had moved back to its original position, and the professor put the mouthpiece and diaphragm in place again, with the stylus resting in the groove made in the foil.

I thought he was about to begin again and say something more. No. The machine was going to talk. The professor took up a piece of stiff cardboard rolled into the shape of a funnel, and placing the small end at the mouthpiece, began to turn the screw as before.

The professor had a half-smile of mingled science and fun on his face, and all the students stood silent, as if something wonderful was about to take place.

There was a faint scratching sound from the funnel, and then, why, then – the machine said, in a shrill and piping voice, 'Mr Charles Barnard has come to see the phonograph. Ha, ha! I do de-c-la-r-e!'.

What could we all do but laugh? It was past belief, too wonderful, too strange and altogether absurd! That the thing should say all that, precisely as the professor had said it, and with a long drawn-out shout at the end of the word 'declare', just as he had shouted at the end! For more than two hours the phonograph recorded every word we spoke into it, and then repeated each word precisely as if the machine had been alive . . .

Can you imagine any more marvellous and wonderful invention? – a machine for recording speech, a machine that will repeat any song or any words in any language and in their proper order, and as many times as you wish. Now if we want to send a message to a friend, we may speak into a phonograph, and make a record of the words in foil. We can then take off the foil and send it to our friend by mail, and he can put the foil on his machine, and then turn the handle and hear every word we said.

Is not this all very strange and funny? Think of a machine that can talk, laugh, sneeze, or sigh, or cry, speak French or German, or even imitate the bark of a dog, or the crow of the morning rooster.

Charles Barnard, ibid.

Under the guardianship of the indefatigable Wayland, 'Mickey' (Michael O'Sullivan, a blind piper from Castlecove, County Kerry) journeyed to Dublin and tied with Denis Delaney for second prize at the *Feis Ceoil* competition in 1899, but not being awarded the first prize, he attributed his ill success to the fairy butter served to him at Mrs Moore's establishment, and also to the malign influence of a dead man's breeches he wore.

It appears that certain members of the Cork Pipers' Club had fitted him out for the occasion with a suit from a 'ready-made' shop, but nothing could convince 'Mickey' that he had not been draped in a dead man's garments. Rather than run any future risks of being 'overlooked', he decided to hasten back to his friends in Kerry; but before setting out on the journey he carefully parcelled up the bewitched breeches and flung it violently into the little shop where it had been purchased, remarking that it was hard for him to take first prize with the fairy butter stuck to him and a dead man's spirit haunting him, or, in other words, 'with God in his heart and the devil in his breeches'.

His guide who accompanied him to Castlecove served in that capacity with him in Kerry, but, having been 'fed up', as they say, and pretty well dressed, he pined for the sound of the Shandon bells and the home allurements beside the 'pleasant water of the Lee'. Lest his youthful guide, blest with perfect eyesight, might go astray, the simple, superstitious, but conscientious, blind piper actually returned with him to Cork.

Obligingly he played his best tunes into an Edison phonograph, but a scowl instead of a smile overspread his handsome features when he heard the machine reproduce the tunes. Evidently regarding this as another instance of the devil's handiwork, he aimed several whacks of his cane at the enchanted box before he could be restrained.

Captain Francis O'Neill,
Irish Minstrels and Musicians, 1913

No tongue I have, no hands, nor yet a voice,
Yet talk or sing or play, which is your choice?
There is no instrument you can name
I am not mistress of; 'tis all the same.
With song I sing untiring with the purest tone,
Soprano, alto, bass or baritone.
All languages are mine; with wond'rous skill
I talk, weep, laugh, and will your senses thrill
With stirring scenes from playwrights – comic, tragic,
All bow in turn to my resistless magic.
Music and song my captives, sound my throne,
I reign supreme, their queen, the Gramophone.

Ladies and gentlemen, I am only, it is true, a gramophone, but I can provide you with an artistic treat such as you could not listen to at any concert in the world. I have with me here that great queen of song, Madame Melba, Signor Caruso, Mischa Elman, John Harrison, Evan Williams and many other distinguished artists. I will now ask you to give me your kind attention . . .

(Here follows a few seconds' silence)

Ladies and gentlemen, I thank you for the kind manner in which you have given me your attention. I also thank you for your generous applause. You must remember that it is not I, a thing of brass and wood, that has been giving you all this pleasure. I am only the vehicle. I have the honour to hold here in my works the living voices of the greatest singers in the world. It is to the actual voices of these great singers that you have been listening. Again, I thank you.

The Gramophone Introducing Itself and Returning Thanks,
10-inch record issued by The Gramophone Company, 1909

THE SOUNDTRACK INVENTED SILENCE

Robert Bresson, *Notes on the Cinematographer*, 1975

The Tape-recorder Reel

I had thought it was the flute-player Gary Hastings who christened this tune in a spirit of post-modernist irony, some time back in the late Seventies: irony, since tape-recorders, if not as compact and ubiquitous as they are now, were readily accessible, and many musicians learned tunes from them; why single out one for special mention? It's not as if it was got from one of those reel-to-reel machines the size of small cardboard suitcases or ladies' vanity cases, that cost as much as a baby Austin car and were a source of wonder to the townland or the neighbourhood. Maybe I'm reading too much into it, but the title seems to have a discernible twist to it, the way a reel can be a 'spool', the bobbin that you wind yarn on; I detect a subtle joke or wind-up. At any rate, I ring up Gary, now Rector of Westport, and Gary tells me that he was playing the tune a couple of weeks ago, but can't remember how it goes now; and besides, it wasn't he who christened it, but someone else. Coincidentally, I had just read that Gary was to play in the interval of the forthcoming Eurovision Song Contest, so we talk some about that . . .

But I digress. In real life, there is no rewind button. Learning a tune in real time is substantially different from having access to its record; it is a dialectic process. You play a tune to someone; you meet him months later, and the tune comes back changed. Sometimes the change is an improvement, a constructive deviation from the known beaten track; sometimes it returns unrecognisable, but none the worse. Or, sitting with someone, you feel your way into the tune, making silent experimental shapes at the bits you haven't got or quite got, till he fills you in with them. Then you try the tune yourself and ask to be corrected. 'Is this the way she goes?' (Tunes, like baby Austins, can be referred to in the feminine gender, though more often by the older generation.) So you go home thinking that you have it, but by the time you've got home, it has all but disappeared. You desperately retain some fragments, some scraps of the blotted aural text you will refer to when you next meet the tune's source. It has become a conversation piece. Or, sometimes, it will resurrect itself unbidden in the inner ear, as something you had always known.

The brain is not a tape-recorder, and it has no recall button. The tape-recorder has no brain, and it has no complex synapses. How often have you been involved in some great session, and some tape-worm has recorded it, and plays it back to you the next day, and it sounds desperate? For the machine is not a human being, and its mike does not know how to filter out extraneous noise. Having no ears, it cannot be attuned to the way the players don't mind being out of tune, since they imagine that they are in tune; their out-of-synch was perfect for the time. The tape-recorder has no soul, no heart. So it would seem; but, trying to establish the nature of 'a record', I turn to *Chambers Dictionary* and learn what I had never known – that it's from the Latin, *recordari*, to get by heart, from *cor, cordis*, the heart. You think you know what words mean, till you find out where they come from, with their many implications and designs; and the branchy family tree of 'record' takes up a whole interesting column in my *Chambers*, which is so well-thumbed it has nearly acquired a thumb-index.

It reminds me that I learned the alphabet by heart, by rote. We singsonged the times-tables. We got songs and poems by heart, by rote; from the Latin *rota*, a wheel, a spool. 'Rote,' says *Chambers*, 'mechanical memory'. Do we learn tunes by rote? Or do we retrace our steps like Ariadne with her spool of thread, escaping from the labyrinth? The LP is a labyrinth of grooves by rote, in which particles of dust can cause the noise to jump into another groove, into the future of its recitation. Its centre turns round like a black lagoon or whirlpool, till the needle drowns in it and sound expires: its time has gone until the next time.

Trying to go back in time, to get back to the ur-source of the concept 'record', I swim down through the flak of folk and rock and jazz, hip-hop, reggae, ska, the easy-listening classics, all the genres, to the first record I ever remember hearing. It must have been around 1961, when I was about thirteen – yes, as old as that, for our family was exceptionally Luddite – and my father had rented a holiday house for a week in Ballyhornan, County Down. It was a whitewashed cottage that adjoined a farm and I remember the warm, fresh, thick, straight-from-the-cow, yellow curd-clotted milk you got in a jug, as different to pasteurised as chalk to cheese.

Somnambulating, drifting through the shades of memory, I walk a hedge-dark aisle in which a strip of sunlit tarmac melts and glistens, past a glimpse in a blackthorn gap of a sudden white-fringed beach, its verging sea of indigo, and I get the ozone whiff beyond the rotting seaweed, then past the cliff-perched radar station with its slowly-scanning, vast Venetian blinds, past the disused filling-station with its rusted wife-and-husband petrol pumps, till the aroma of the farmyard hits me with the chickenshit and cowclaps I negotiate *en route*, a pong of hay and tractor diesel, oozings of the ozone once again, and the smell of milk and silage, till I arrive and click the half-door latch and walk into the cool interior of damp and Calor gas, the way my father, later, struck a match and cupped it as he held it to the mantle, and it popped and flared and settled to a steady bright yellow hiss; then I proceeded through the household to the outside wooden loo, the Sanisan, redolent with sweet chemicals and human dung, then, afterwards, I walked the brick path to the creaking back door as a sudden cool wind blew that drew me to the gaslit chiaroscuro dark where shadows loomed beyond my parents as they settled for a game of cards we all would join in, and afterwards again, my father cranked the wind-up gramophone that smelled of oil and pencil-boxes. The record paten is put on devotedly, experimentally, with unsure reverence: 'China Doll', by Slim Whitman:

> I'm tired of cry-ee-ay-ee-ing
> And no-good sigh-ee-ay-ee-ing
> That's why I'm buying
> My china doll . . .

The yodel in it brought to mind incongruous images, full of holes as a Swiss cheese: among the alpenhorns and cuckoo clocks, cowbells clunked and donged like angeluses gone awry. Pebbles tinkled in the icy streams. I had not seen *The Sound of Music* then, but we acquired its sound-track years later to accompany the new mahogany-veneered radiogram that resided in the front room, more furniture than instrument, like a distant cousin of the china-cabinet. Nevertheless, it was a serious piece of equipment with speakers the size of meat-safes. It had a full growly bass and a meticulous clear treble and the ornaments would buzz and shiver on their glass shelves when you turned it up full blast.

We called our front room the 'parlour', though there was little *parler* in it; it was more a place for lonely contemplation. In my late teens I'd sit there in the melancholic happiness or gloom of unrequited love and listen to Moura Lympany playing Chopin's *Études*. I was going through my cultured phase, though never quite abandoning the folk. I played Joan Baez too:

> Don't sing love songs, you'll wake my mother
> She's sleeping here right by my side
> And in her right hand a silver dagger
> She says that I can't be your bride . . .

Then I discovered the great *sean-nós* singers Nioclás Tóibín and Joe Heaney with their desolate songscapes of doomed lovers wandering on mountainsides, their paths occasionally crossing before they separate forever; and there is a small dark gap at the end of the song through which you glimpse the glimmering terrain of Connemara or wherever, swept by shadows of the nimbostratus. The human figures have receded to their separate households, where they sit up all night, everyone in bed but them, and they tend the low glow of the turf.

You got four of these songs on the Gael-Linn EP format, and you played them over and over; for, though I am sometimes inclined to argue against the fidelity of records, their disembodied medium is somehow appropriate to the *sean-nós* and its lonely desolation. When the singer sings, her vision is turned inward and outward to the interlocking terrain of the song. She may be urged on and encouraged by the present circumstances, but she is separate as a singer, and for now, only she knows how to find the pathway to the other world. Those who hold and wind her hands do so as if across a great abyss. That is why the last words of the song are often spoken, reassurance that the singer has come back to the everyday and is willing to converse in speech. After the applause, normal time is resumed and conversation breaks out. Drink is ordered furiously and the electronic cash-register sends out a flurry of pre-recorded digital bleeps. Then there is a

Chinese-whisper diatribe of hushes as *ciuneas* – 'quiet' or 'order' – is restored.

I am engaged by how the singer penetrates this order of quiet, how a breathing space can be made for the song. Listening to Darach Ó Catháin singing, say, '*Caiptín Ó Máille*', I become aware of how he paces it and phrases it and makes little melismatic bridges between gaps, or shifts the place where the gap should be and walks across it nonchalantly. He organises time and space within a set of ground rules, and then goes against them subtly when the need arises, for the song has a deep broad structure in which many different mental pathways can be taken. The song has many readings and interpretations, and behind it is a story or a commentary:

brí, 'the force, meaning'
míníu, 'the explanation' ⎫ *an amhráin*, 'of the song'
údar, 'the authority, justification' ⎭

as the Irish terminology has it. Tim Robinson, cartographer and author, has a story behind the song which is too good to leave out here:

Captain O'Malley

The famous smuggler Captain George O'Malley, *an Caiptín Máilleach* or *Caiptín Ó Máille*, as he is known in Irish, was born in 1786, in an area called Ballynakill, the village of the church, in the remote north-western corner of Connemara. Its coastline was designed by nature with smugglers in mind; its deep and winding inlets run to the foot of the trackless mountains. George's earliest memory, according to his own account, was of watching his father's sloop sailing into Ballynakill Bay hotly pursued by the coastguards in their cutter. Of course old O'Malley knew every inch of the coast, and he was able to turn suddenly and dart through a narrow passage between an islet and the shore, and head out to sea again, leaving the coastguard cutter to blunder on into the bay and run itself aground on a sandbank – whereupon O'Malley magnanimously came back and threw them a rope, and hauled them off the sand; they were so appreciative of his gallantry that they shook his hand and asked no questions about his cargo –

tobacco, wines and brandy from Guernsey. Ballynakill, remote as could be from any centre of authority, flourished in those days; the O'Malley girls wore amazing French and Spanish hats and silk dresses. It was not until the 1820s that roads were built into Connemara from Galway, opening it to the forces of law – and the roads were therefore blamed for the economic decline of the area. Two and three hundred years earlier the O'Malleys had been the dominant clan of the Mayo coast, a little further north; a seafaring people, of whom it was said that there never was an O'Malley who wasn't a good sailor. In the 16th century the greatest of them all, Grace O'Malley, commanded a fleet of galleys and was regarded by Queen Elizabeth's statesmen in Ireland as a 'notorious feminine sea-pirate', a force to be conciliated. In one of the boastful songs our hero George O'Malley wrote about himself, he says, '*Is mise Seoirse Ó Máille, fear maith de bhunadh Ghráinne*' – I am George O'Malley, a good man of Grace O'Malley's line.

Young George equipped himself to follow his father into the smuggler's trade, by joining the crew of a coastguard vessel; after some time with her he knew every detail of the coastguards' operations, and had seen for himself that the Guernsey sloops could outsail the Revenue cutters. Then for some years he led a wildly adventurous life around the world's seaways; whether the tales he brought back are all true or not, I wouldn't like to swear. He ships on a boat from Dublin to Oporto; in the streets of Glasgow he is seized by a pressgang and finds himself an unwilling member of the English navy, in a convoy to Lisbon – this is the period of the Napoleonic Wars. He jumps ship and is recaptured, he sees action in the North Sea, taking Danish ships as prizes; he escapes again from his ship when it puts in at Leith in Scotland, he sells his trousers and walks to Glasgow, and ships on a trader to the West Indies. Later on he is on his way to Cadiz when his ship is taken by a French privateer, he and the rest of the crew are made prisoner and taken to the Tower of St Malo, from whence they are marched to Cambray in the Netherlands – it takes them three months. After three years in prison there they are marched in chains 250 miles to the Austrian frontier – it is the winter of 1812: Napoleon in retreat from Moscow and his empire crumbling, and no-one seems to know what to do with the prisoners. He goes mad, is released, is succoured by some nuns, and as soon as he is recovered, which seems to take only a day or two, he gets a berth on a convoy ship to Madeira and the Windward Islands. In the Caribbean he becomes a pirate, against his will. A group of his shipmates come into his cabin one day – he is a mate by this time – and tell him that they have heard that they could lease a vessel in New York for a season of piracy, and they want him to be their captain; in fact they insist. George is shocked at this suggestion; he reads them a sermon on their Christian duties, but he ends it by saying that since they outnumber him he'll agree to their request. So they lease the ship, they have a very successful season, and they are sailing back to New York laden down with plunder when they are jumped on by a bigger pirate vessel, and lose the lot. Disillusioned, he comes home to take up the family business. After a prosperous career he is persuaded to give up smuggling, and writes his memoirs – they've never been published, but at some date someone made a typescript of them which I have seen – seven fat volumes of flimsy paper, a lot of it unreadably verbose. Captain O'Malley ended his days in the workhouse at Westport, where he died in about 1864.

Two songs attributed to the captain are still sung in Connemara; one of them in praise of his boat, the other in praise of himself.

So, Darach walks the line between the story and the song:

An fharraige gur ghéim sí agus las na tonnta tréana
Ó chriothnaigh na spéartha agus mhéadaigh ar an gceo
'S dhá mbeadh caint ag na clára go n-inseoidís scéal cráite
An ghaireacht is chuaigh an bás dhúinn 's gan eadrainn ach iad.

The howling sea leaped up and brutal waves exploded
O the skies rained down through thickening fog
And if the planks could speak they'd tell a tortured tale
How only they had been between us and our deaths.

And *Darach* means, in Irish, 'firm as an oak', this intervening hull between us and the deep Atlantic, where the connotation 'thick as a plank' is, for once, not pejorative but is shaped and crafted as the song is put together by a master shipwright or a smuggler. For it is the singer's job to infiltrate the system; the song is contraband. He has to know the times and tides and when an underwater reef will have sufficient water over it. He has to climb to the top of the mast to study the contours of the sea floor and their isobar configurations. Standing at the helm, he becomes a steering apparatus. Eternally, he hauls ropes through blocks.

Agus tá mo lámha stróicthe go síoraí 'g tarraingt rópaí
Tá an croiceann 'gus an fheoil siad tarraingthe 'mach ón gcnáimh
Ach más é an bás a gheall Mac Dé dhúinn cé'n maith a bheith
*   dhá shéanadh*
Ach a ghabháil go Flaitheas Dé dhúinn in aon stáid amháin.

And my hands are torn from eternally hauling ropes
And the skin and the flesh pulled clean from the bone
But if the Son of God has decreed our death, what use to offer
    our denial
For we can only go to Heaven, united in the eyes of God.

The long note of exile runs through this song, as it does in the love songs, and we sense Darach Ó Catháin's powerful identification with them. Born in Leitir Mór in Connemara, he moved, at the age of nine, to Rath Cairn in County Meath. Here the Irish Government had acquisitioned a tract of land in the Thirties and had transplanted Irish-speaking families in an attempt to improve the lot of the language. However, Darach left in the Sixties to work in Leeds, and remained there until his death on 29 September 1989, exiled twice over.

It is arguable that Darach's style of singing is one which has not changed substantially for centuries; but of course the tradition is not wholly static, and Darach collaborated with the late Seán Ó Riada in his attempts to redefine Irish music. In contemporary Connemara, the *sean-nós* genre co-exists with other kinds of music, just as its macaronic landscape includes hacienda-style bungalows and 'genuine' thatched cottages. 'Country' music is big here, as it is throughout Ireland, with the interesting twist that a new hybrid of Irish language Country has evolved, as sung by Na hAncairí ('The Anchors', or, possibly, 'The Hermits', as in 'anchorite') and other groups. If Country is a state of mind, Connemara has extended its borders.

All I Ever

Country and Western music – 'Country', to its devotees – is often
accused of being mawkish, maudlin and banal. It sometimes is, and
so is opera; but I think the criticism misses the point that the genre
is *dependent* on cliché and on stock scenarios and phrases. If 'stock'
at one point in its history meant a tree-trunk, it is augmented by a
family tree of branching limbs and leafy ornament; and if 'cliché' was
a stereotype plate or a bank of type, then an impression taken from
it can come out freshly-minted as an original print. Ralph Stanley's
and Ricky Skaggs's rendition of Dorothy Skaggs's 'All I Ever Loved
Was You' is a case in point:

> All I ever loved was you.
> You broke a heart that cried for you.
> I've wasted all my tears on you.
> For all I ever loved was you.
>
> Go out and find somebody new.
> But you'll be sorry if you do.
> You'll never find a love so true.
> For all I ever loved was you.
>
> All I ever loved was you.
> You broke a heart that cried for you.
> I've wasted all my tears on you.
> For all I ever loved was you.
>
> Buy him rings and diamonds too.
> And tell him that your love is true.
> I'm sure he'll learn a lesson too.
> For all I ever loved was you.

All I ever loved was you.
You broke a heart that cried for you.
I've wasted all my tears on you.
For all I ever loved was you.

For all I ever loved was you.

From *Saturday Night & Sunday Morning*,
Freeland Recording Co. Inc., 1992

This is cliché driven to distraction. A lot of Country songs have this same basic short format of two verses – sometimes only one – and a chorus: 'All I Ever Loved Was You' stretches reiteration to near breaking-point. But it's held together by that very glue of you/new/do/true/too/you, and by the singers' total commitment to the song, their dwelling on the sobbing assonances with their smoky dual voice. It puts me in mind of this animated feature I saw once, which consisted simply of a cartoon-figure man saying 'I love you' in about a hundred and eighty different ways, investing them with shades of love or hate or dubiousness, and accompanying them with the appropriate histrionic gestures, till we realised the huge and bronchial possibilities of what his oxymoron love might be.

Making songs like 'All I Ever Loved Was You' is a kind of Zen discipline, where the line between the simple and banal is very thin. It is a highly artificial construct, but is underwritten by assumptions of the authenticity of universal feelings, as embodied in the speech of common beings. Country is rural, and would be endorsed by William Wordsworth, if we believe his preface to his *Lyrical Ballads*:

Low and rustic life was generally chosen, because in that condition, the essential passions of the heart find a better soil in which they can attain their maturity, are under less restraint, and speak a plainer and more authentic language; because in that condition of life our elementary feelings co-exist in a state of greater simplicity, and, consequently, may be more accurately contemplated, and more forcibly communicated; because the manners of rural life germinate from those elementary feelings; and, from the necessary character of rural occupations, are more easily comprehended; and are more durable; and, lastly, because in that condition the passions of men are incorporated with the beautiful and permanent forms of nature.

Of course, the language of this manifesto runs directly counter to its thesis; and Wordsworth's attempts at the ballad genre were a mixed bag; sometimes his greatest hits occurred when he went against his own rules, and stuck a big word in amongst the plainer registers:

> No motion has she now, no force;
> She neither hears nor sees,
> Rolled round in earth's diurnal course
> With rocks and stones and trees . . .

And Dorothy Wordsworth might have approved the nerve of Dorothy Skaggs, for writing simply is not easy. The words must emerge from a deep awareness of all the floating lines and verses that inhabit songs like these, flitting through the centuries and reverberating in the mouths of generations; and the maker must surrender herself to that authority. She must walk the thin line stretched above the chasm of the past. The poet Michael Longley has said that if poets were tightrope walkers, then many of them would be dead; Dorothy Skaggs, then, is an Olympic Olga Korbut on the beam. Economy and elegance, where the absolutely end-stopped lines provide a musical and contemplative space within the mantra of the words. Grace under pressure, that kind of thing, where the pressure comes from the almost-unbearably-repeated, ululating moan of 'you'; and somehow, 'you' becomes a near impersonal, a second person singular. It is measured against the forlorn 'I', who is yet so confident in his or her decree of love, as they revel in its unrequitedness. I say his or her, because the song is a bit of a gender-bender. Written by a woman, sung by two men, the third stanza is crucial:

> Buy him rings and diamonds too.
> And tell him that your love is true.

If I understand the conventions of real country life, guys are not bought rings and diamonds. No, it is they who do the buying, and I am nearly sure that Dorothy Skaggs would have sung:

> Buy her rings and diamonds too.
> And tell her that your love is true.

because it is a woman's song. So, men singing it must reverse the real
life convention and adopt the convention of the song; for in Country
songs, men must speak as Countrymen.

I forgot to mention the instrumental break of fiddle, mandoline
and guitar which comes in just after this crux, as if the guys wanted
to relax and contemplate, as we do, all the implications of such
single-minded *doppelgänger* love. The break, of course, is nothing
like a jazz break: it is the tune of the song repeated with some tiny
melodic variations. It gives you literal breathing space between the
relentless lyrics.

The dead white European male music critic, Constant Lambert,
has remarked that 'the whole trouble with a folk song is that once
you have played it through there is nothing much to do except play
it over again and play it rather louder'; this might well apply to a
classically-arranged piano piece, but is singularly inappropriate to real
folk song. For there is no score: you must know the song by heart, and
sing it from the heart, so it comes out different every time. As you
renew that feeling each time that you sing or play it, you discover new
progressions, new negotiations of the known route. The song must *be*.
It must be sung right *now*, contemporaneously; it does not know the
printed confines of the dotted crotcheted page. It is an emblem of
its many possibilities; there is no one known way of singing it, since
what you knew before will not be what you know tomorrow. There
is no trouble with folk song, except its inexhaustibility.

At present, my memory for songs is not what it used to be; maybe
it never was. I am embarrassed by how many songs I used to sing, and
now forget. Could I sing all the songs I used to sing – an archaeology
of all the palimpsests – I'm sure the catalogue would run well into
three figures. As I write, I come up with this emaciated list:

Love is Teasing
McCafferty
The Wild Colonial Boy
Blackwater Side
The Rambling Boys of Pleasure
Baile Uí Liagh
Máirín de Barra
The Mickey Dam
Derry Harbour
An Sceilpín Draighneach

My Boy Willie
Polly-Wolly-Doodle
Irene, Goodnight
She Moves through the Fair

And that's about it. There are very many scraps and fragments floating around between the mental synapses, and some big near-complete chunks of songs; and it's possible I could resurrect a good score if I put my mind to it, but if asked to sing them at the drop of a hat, I'd be bound to stumble or to freeze. Yet I know they're all there, embedded in the memory bank like clichés in a printer's shop, where he leaves inky fingerprints behind as grooved recordings of his presence. I don't sing them now simply because I don't sing them. The songs demand a context of being sung, of having listeners and other singers round you. You need that feedback. You have to be in the way of singing songs.

Len Graham, who sings more or less professionally, reckons he has about 200 songs at present, and could work up some scores more if challenged; but even in his case, the repertoire evolves and shifts as new songs are taken on board and others get lost. And because I don't sing out as much as I used to, and haven't done so for many years, I've lost the songs. Songs are nothing if there is no audience, though sometimes, in a bathroom echo-mode, the audience might be yourself.

Of these few songs I sing at present, two remain from my childhood – 'My Boy Willie', which I heard from my grandma and my father, and 'The Wild Colonial Boy', which I'm sure they sang as well. Here it is, as I transcribed it in my school song book, some thirty-seven years ago:

THE WILD COLONIAL BOY

There was a wild Colonial Boy
Jack Dougan was his name
He was born and bred in Ireland
In a place called Castlemaine
He was his father's only son
His mother's pride and joy
And dearly did his parents love
The Wild Colonial Boy.

II

At the early age of sixteen years
He ran away from home
And to Australia's sunny shores
He was inclined to roam
He robbed the rich and helped the poor
He stabbed James McEvoy
A terror to Australia was
The Wild Colonial Boy

III

One morning on the prairie wide
Jack Dougan rode along
Listening to a mocking bird
Singing its mocking song
Up jumped three troopers fierce and wild,
Kelly, Davies and Fitzroy
They had all set out to capture him,
The Wild Colonial Boy.

IV

"Surrender in the Queen's name,
For we are three to one.
Surrender in the Queen's name
For you're a plundering son"
Jack drew two pistols from his side
And proudly waved them high.
"I'll fight but not surrender", cried
The Wild Colonial Boy.

V

He fired a shot at Kelly
Which brought him to the ground
He fired a shot at Davies
Which felled him at the sound.
But a bullet pierced his brave young heart
From the pistol of Fitzroy.
And that was how they captured him,
The Wild Colonial Boy.

I note, with the embarrassed eye of hindsight, that apostrophe in 'parent's', and tell myself it must have been a Freudian slip of the pen, an unconscious follow-up from 'father's' and 'mother's'. More interestingly, I am made aware of the subtle osmotic changes which have crept into the text: I now sing 'He left his native home', not 'He ran away from home' — two entirely different propositions, with their different hints of resignation or rebellion; 'Judge McEvoy', not 'James', which, depending on your politics, might be more politically correct; and, most crucially, 'Up jumped three troopers', not 'Up jumped three troopers fierce and wild' — I had simply forgotten what class of troopers these were, and to make my truncated version fit the tune, I'd make a little glottal stop after 'jumped', and elongate the 'three troopers',* ending in a glottal colon, all of which gave, I must have thought unconsciously, a dramatic onomatopoeic contour to the line.

Looking at them now, and singing them in to myself, I don't know which is better; but the question of choice has given the song a new, uncertain dimension and it will never be the same again because it never was. Similarly, I have 'murdering son', but like the original 'plundering' better, with its implication that the troopers reckoned this to be the most heinous epithet in their vocabulary of troopers' curses.

I realise, too, that I've changed the air somewhat, inebriating it with that of a variant, 'The Bold Jack Donaghue', which recounts a career so similar that Dougan and Donaghue must be 'aka's for each other. Both sets of words and airs cross currents, till you find yourself in midstream, and, going with the flow, produce a hybrid. The song is always open to negotiation. Trying to find a pitch to sing it in, you cannot use a constant pitchpipe. There is no written pitch. You have to sound it out, and how you do depends on the circumstances: on the state of your lungs and vocal cords and diaphragm and larynx; on the state of the room or the stage or the hotel foyer; on the state of the audience; on the state of your brain; on what went before and what might come after; on what you've eaten or drunk or smoked; on the relative humidity and temperature; on all the tiny algebraic connections that make up the space where songs are mediated.

You might pitch a song low in the intimate surrounds of a back kitchen in the small hours, where you know there will be hush and

---

* Nicholas Carolan's mother sang 'Up jumped three mounted troopers'.

quiet; you might pitch it high in a jam-packed pub where hubbub circumvents you and you want or try to cut through the smoke and buzz of talk; or, in the same jammed circumstances, you might sing it conversationally into another's hand-cupped ear, as you cup your own ear so that you might hear the song-transference process as it comes from your interior into another's brain. That is why it is anathema to transcribe songs in fixed key signatures. There are no keys in folk song, for the concept of the lock does not exist. There is no perfect pitch. There is, instead, a latch, its thumb-scoop polished by the common touch of generations. Offering easy access, the latch still has an etiquette attached to it: you might, for instance, jiggle it before you enter someone's kitchen, to give the someone warning, so that they can welcome you and say, 'Sure just walk right on in'; you might cough, or knock, according to the closeness or remoteness of your kinship patterns. The phrasing of your latch-work, like a digital thumb-print, is embedded in the memory of your hosts, and they will know you in advance, the way they know the pattern of your footsteps like an echo:

> We heard a strange sound in the Bainriggs' wood as we were floating on the water. It *seemed* in the wood, but it must have been above it, for presently we saw a raven very high above us – it called again and again as it flew onwards, and the mountains gave back the sound, seeming as if from their center a musical bell-like answering to the bird's hoarse voice. We heard both the call of the bird and the echo after we could see him no longer.
>
> Dorothy Wordsworth, *The Grasmere Journals*

That reiterated raven-call puts me in mind of Hank Williams' 'lonesome whippoorwill'; of lonesome freight trains crying in the night; of Edgar Allan Poe; of William Wordsworth's 'To the Cuckoo' ('. . . shall I call thee bird,/Or but a wandering voice?'); of daffodils; of 'in vacant or in pensive mood'; of how the newly-unrequited lover wants the past back; of how the past returns in vivid glimpses; and of Skaggs and Stanley, singing 'All I Ever Loved Was You'. It is the landscape of a song, full of resonant mnemonics; and 'Country' is a state of mind.

Country Roads

I am looking for a diary – for the year 1972, I think – in which the only entry is a few days spent in Arranmore Island off the coast of Donegal; and as I try to remember what I wrote (the diary refuses to locate itself), bits of landscape start to come back through the fog. It was a cloudless Easter. As we crossed over, the boat sailed on its own reflection through the green glass water. And the island itself, as we approached it, brooded on its hazy mirror image: a labyrinth of stone walls, derelict potato drills and tattered barbed wire fences marking extinct boundaries; dazzling oblong whitewashed houses scattered randomly in anticlines and scarps; and in the near interior, pyramids of rusted cans and cars, glacial desolations of erratic stones, littered hill-slopes; clouds of sheep that might be stone.

Among the dilapidated dwellings, there were some that had their roofs more or less intact: we wandered into one and found some sticks of furniture, bits of crockery still on the kitchen table, and a dead mouse visibly embalmed in an empty milk-bottle. The calendar read 1955. We touched the untouched dust and left our fingerprints behind, for every inch of Arranmore is written on and spoken for, transformed by human hand and voice: the island is a record of itself. Little roads of dirt and broken limestone wander mazily around and up the gradients, leading nowhere, it would seem, till they arrive at somewhere – a disused peat-bog, a mountain pool, a lighthouse – or peter out because there's nowhere else to go, and mark the site of someone else's lost endeavour.

Meandering between the past and present, disappearing, then discovering themselves again, these routes suggest linguistic parallels. Here, the Irish and the English languages are locked in debate, and Irish is losing ground: although the island is officially designated as a *Gaeltacht*, it is more accurately a *breac-Gaeltacht* – literally, speckled *Gaeltacht*; pockets of Donegal tweed Irish among the broad overlapping patches of English. It is a ravelled hank of various yarns: in one household, the parents will speak English to the children and Irish among themselves; in another, it is vice versa; in yet others, the children have long gone to America, and write home at ever-lengthening intervals. Whatever is spoken, these linguistic kinships alter once a stranger walks across their threshold; often, where a dwelling has two doors, the front door is the back.*

Littered with abandoned cars and turf-stacks, it is a macaronic landscape. In the pub that night, two men debate the Irish word for 'the wake of a boat on the ebb tide'. Or rather, it is early morning, for the pub keeps no hours. Beyond the ordinance of clock time, an old woman sings an old song that is new to me. It is a macaronic song:

> Yesterday morning, *ar maidin inné*
> I spied a young damsel, *is thug me dí spéis*
> *D'fhiostruigh mé den bhruinneall,* but she went away
> *Is d'fhág sí faoi bhrón mé,* I'm sorry to say.

> *Is trua gan mé is í* straight going away
> *Ar dtriall san loing adaidh* over yon sea
> *Gan fios ag aonduine* where we were going to stay
> *A Rí nár dheas an dóigh é* should I live but one day.

It seems typical of the genre that it is playful and light: tongue in cheek, or two tongues in one cheek: *double entendre.* Her songs wholly in Irish, on the other hand, have a direct sweet melancholy:

> *Is fada mé a ghrá, ag dúil is ag fuireacht leat,*
> *Is iomdha sin tráth a chaith mé san turas seo,*
> *Nó ar fhuaraigh do dháimh ó chonnaic mé roimhe thú,*
> *Tá mé 'mo chodhladh, 's má tá níl néal.*

---

* The front and back of these cottages were the same; the two doors were opposite one another, and which was in use depended on the way the wind was blowing.

(For far too long, my love, I hoped and waited for you
Through all the episodes before our journey's end;
But since I saw you last you have gone cold;
I am sleeping now, and it's no dream.)

Or, from another song:

Tá mé 'mo shuí ó d'éirigh an ghealach aréir
Ag cur teineadh síos gan sgíth, is dá fadú go géar;
Tá bunadh an tí 'na luí is tá mise liom fhéin;
Tá na coiligh ag glaíodh is an tír 'na gcodhladh ach mé.

(I have sat up since the moon rose late last night
Coaxing the fire to hold on to the last bit of heat;
The household are all abed and I am all alone;
The cocks are crowing, and the whole world is asleep, except for
me.)

And afterwards, we stagger homewards through the mists of
dawn.

New Year's Eve 1979: Belfast-Donegal

Patches of dense fog: driving on to the Ml slipway from Belfast, we
are stopped by a UDR patrol; we recognise them by their uniform.
The usual questions: who are we? Where are we going? Where are
we coming from? Why? We are Pádraigín Ní Uallacháin, Deirdre
Shannon, and myself, and we are going to spend a few days in
Glencolmcille in Donegal; why exactly, I don't know; it must have
been an escape or a holiday. So we were giving the usual answers
when out of the fog – goose-stepping, saluting – appeared this little
old man shouting *clé, deas, clé, deas* (left, right, left, right) in clear
Donegal Irish, marching up the hyphenated white line, vanishing
momentarily and then returning.

–*Bhfuil sibh ag dul go Tír Chonaill?*
–Are you going to the land of Conall (i.e. Donegal)?

Irish is not, by and large, the language of Belfast; but this was his lucky day. To cut a long story short, we took him to Donegal, together with the few belongings he had gathered together in a plastic shopping bag – old newspapers, an empty chocolate box with a picture of a dog on it, a battered copy of an LP called *Country Roads* by Philomena Begley and Her Ramblin' Men:

> *Country roads take me home*
> *To the place where I belong . . . .*
> *The radio reminds me of my home so far away . . .*

He kept coming back to the song between snippets of dislocated conversation.

And part of Condy O'Connell's story – he did not choose to divulge it all – was that he had been a bomber pilot in the Second World War. He had been shot down behind enemy lines, himself and his co-pilot. They had emerged alive. They had wandered for days through hedges, ditches, along broken railway lines; eventually they reached a *Luftwaffe* fighter base. They stole an enemy plane and just as they were taking off, says Condy,

> *Throw out them carpets, says I to my co-pilot –*
> *What carpets, says he, he didn't understand she'd never lift*
> *With all that weight of carpets in her, but he did as he was bid*
> *And she soared like a bird across the enemy lines*
> *And flew like any swallow*
> *And landed clean and safe in Ranafast.*

I had a momentary recollected glimpse of Ranafast: a glitter of bog-pools, tiny boulder-strewn fields, a winding road of broken limestone, a wind-swept single tree. But we were nearly in Enniskillen; time to stop for a drink and a sandwich.

The New Year's Eve Hunt party had just arrived in the pub: red coats, black hats, loud anglified accents, everyone standing around in a loose assertion of territorial rights; these were owners of land, or their sons and daughters. Condy approached one of the girls:

> –*I seen you; I seen you in Hyde Park in London.*
> –*But you must be mistaken, my good man.*

–No, I seen you all right, standing on a soap-box; preaching that the rich should give their land to the poor.

Afterwards, he made friends with a black-and-tan terrier dog not unlike the dog on the chocolate box.

It had been a long day. And now, crossing the border at Pettigo, he was starting to fall asleep. The road began to climb and twist and narrow: we were in Donegal. Dark mountains and baroque clouds swayed beyond the aisle of light thrown by the headlamps.

Country roads take me home
To the place where I belong . . .

His voice trailed off into silence. Nearly home.

Hallowe'en 1982: Teelin, County Donegal

It is the morning after the night before and snatches of the night before – fiddle tunes, hubbub, the clink of glasses – keep filtering through from the memory-bank. We are driving out to the coast to clear our heads – or rather, *up* to the coast, towards Slieve League, the highest sea-cliff in Western Europe, following this precipitous erratic mountain road that winds between stone walls, potato drills, stone-littered patchy fields, one man idling over a spade who raises his hand in an understated rhetoric of hail or farewell, and the clouds piled high between mountains, while these fiddle tunes keep coming back insistently, hectic, passionate and melancholic; half-remembered fragments. The bits and pieces of the landscape sidle into place, accommodated by the loops and spirals of the road, its meditated salients and inclines: and now, as at other times, I wonder if the disciplined wildness of Donegal music has anything to do with this terrain. For nature, here, is never wholly pristine or untouched: the land is possessed and repossessed, named, forgotten, lost and rediscovered; it is under constant dispute; even in its dereliction, it implies a human history. A line of a sentimental song comes back to me: 'Sure your hearts are like your mountains, in the homes of Donegal'. Presumably, the writer intended that we read 'big' for 'mountains'; yet mountains are also hard and stony; they are barriers to be circumvented or defeated. In Donegal fiddle music, this unconscious irony is transformed into purposeful energy.

It is a music of driving, relentless rhythm that teeters on the edge of falling over itself; it seems to almost overtake itself, yet reins in at the brink. A jagged melodic line is nagging at me as we arrive at a high promontory. The sea appears from nowhere. On the right, the immense absurd precipice of Slieve League falls into a tiny silent line of foam, some rocks. How far away is it? The eye has nothing to scale: a human figure, if you could imagine it against this, would be lost; that seagull hovering over there is either miles away, or just within reach. Turning back to the sea again, you can hear it, if you listen very closely: a vast lonesome whispering that stretches all the way to North America.

Fiddlin' John's Big Gobstopper

In this film about the people of the Appalachian Mountains there is a man who believes that only he, in the whole wide world, has found God. He sits on a swing seat on his porch, holding a hickory switch. God speaks through the antenna of the switch. The man holds it in his hands and asks it questions; it answers with a nod or quiver as it bends and listens to the source. It is his divining rod. He lives in a rusted corrugated-tin shack surrounded by a junk-strewn yard. He keeps the radio switched off except for the news, the happenings which give him intimations of Armageddon. For otherwise the radio brings music, the Devil's music, sin made audible.

Then there are the faith-healers, the speakers of tongues, the handlers of snakes, the drinkers of strychnine, who believe the Word has rendered them immune. Some of them allow music, but not the Devil's dance music, which overpowers you with jump and rhythm. The camera pans through a landscape of derelict farms and dirt roads and automobile graveyards and clapboard faith missions, till we at last get a glimpse of this Devil-music. The film crew has assembled a band on a mountain-side: an old fiddler in his seventies or eighties, and what look like various members of his extended family – a son, perhaps, playing a five-string banjo; maybe his cousin, playing an unorthodox style of bottle-neck guitar, left-handed, with the bottle-neck the 'wrong' way round; and two girls* in their thirties or forties, one playing a washboard,

* 'Girl', latterly, has become the subject of a politically correct debate. In Ireland, the word is often used by women in referring to themselves, not disparagingly but to imply strength and individuality of character. I had the good fortune to be present when the great Tyrone singer Sarah Ann O'Neill first met the great Louth singer Mary Ann Carolan. She recognised her as a kindred spirit, for after Mrs Carolan had sung, Sarah Ann stood up and said, 'That girl there that just sung, would she sing another?' Mrs Carolan was in her seventies.

the other a broomstick one-string bass.

The fiddle-player holds the fiddle in the crook of his arm; his face is expressionless, deadpan. They are all expressionless, except for the disciplined energy of their hands. The energy comes from the line of the music, a force without crescendo or diminuendo; it follows its line until it finishes. If this is the Devil's music, then the Devil is a pragmatist: while the music exists, there is nothing better; it does not strive for a perfect state, nor intimate the sublime, but runs within an acceptance of the world as it is; it is true to what people are, and absolutely true to the musicians who are playing it. There is no deception, there are no histrionics, no acting-out of unfelt emotion. Because of these values, folk music is often perceived to be 'impersonal'; and the producers of the film seem to accord with this view, for the musicians, at the end of it all, are given no credit. They have become anonymous, or they are illustrations of a theme. The implication is that they are hillbillies, and one hillbilly is much the same as another.

So far as I know, these people do not call themselves 'hillbillies'; nor is their music so called, but is generally referred to as 'Old-time', or 'Old-timey'. I love Old-time music, but it is almost unperceived in Britain and Ireland, where it is thought to be 'Bluegrass'. Even in the USA its audience is limited: in a record store in Mount Airy, North Carolina – one of the centres of Old-time – I found some dozen tapes of this music among a hundred or so of Blue-grass. I bought the whole dozen, much to the bemusement of the owner. When he discovered I was Irish, he was even more perplexed.

Old-time has, it seems, redneck Dixie connotations which sit uncomfortably with the overriding commercialism of most American music. It is not music to be consumed, but to be played and danced to. Here, unlike Bluegrass, instrumental breaks are rare. The players start the tune together, and they stay together, and they all play the same tune a lot of times; yet each time round the tune is subtly different – not, perhaps, because the musicians make conscious variations, but because they play the tune that very way at that very time, and it is exactly true to life, which has no pre-determined score, but goes on from one split second to the next, driving through the now into the future. *Hillbilly*? Its sophistication is immense.

If Old-timey has frills, they are subliminal: little bowed grace notes, say, which lean into the rhythm; for the rhythm is the thing, which absolutely fulfils the music's purpose. Its purpose is to close the gap between the dancers and the dance; yet its wildness summons up the mountain-gaps and airy distances between the scattered settlements of Appalachia. It has a high lonesome note, a floating *cri de coeur* that longs to find a partner. It makes you want to dance.

I want to hear it so much that I rummage around and find one of the tapes I bought in Mount Airy. This is the Iron Mountain String Band:

Iron Mountain String Band
'Music From The Mountain'

The Iron Mountain String Band is a traditional, Old-time dance band. Their sound is powerful and driving, yet graceful and smooth. They are often seen at Southern music contests and at dances. The music on this tape is a good example of the pure Grayson County style which is still alive. We hope you will enjoy it.

Nancy Bethel • Bass. Along with her husband, Nick, Nancy has played traditional music for years. The Bethels' outgoing hospitality is well known to those familiar with old time music competitions. Like the congeniality shown in the Bethel camp, Nancy's bass playing reflects the necessary give-and-take which makes up an Old-time band. Nancy is a resident of Selma, Virginia.

Gene Hall • Guitar. Gene is the band's manager and co-ordinator. He gave the band its name because he lives near Iron Mountain and sees it every morning on his way to work. Gene's guitar playing reflects the image of the mountain – solid, strong and dependable. He lives with his wife, Anna Lee (a very fine spoon-player and flatfoot dancer), in the Elk Creek Community of Grayson County.

Enoch Rutherford • Clawhammer Banjo. Enoch is well known for his pure, hard-driving, Grayson County banjo playing. His style clearly reflects his home community's name of Gold Hill in that, like gold, it is now very rare. Over the years Enoch has performed with the areas's best musicians. He has also been generous about passing along the tradition.

W.S. Mayo • Fiddle. W.S. (Wiley) employs a unique under-handed Grayson County style of bowing which he learned from the late Albert Hash. He has always enjoyed playing Old-time dance tunes with other traditional musicians. Like the other band members, he is well known to be ready to play all day and all night. W.S. lives in Glade Spring, Virginia with his wife, Ray (who also plays clawhammer banjo).

Dale Morris • Vocals. Dale is a well known and versatile local musician. Because of his natural feel and ear for traditional tunes, he is a great friend of Old-time musicians. He has graciously agreed to help the Iron Mountain String Band with the production and vocals of this tape. Dale lives in the Elk Creek Community with his family.

So I stick it into the sound system, and I'm writing this and tapping my feet to the great music when my four-year-old daughter, Mary, comes into the kitchen and starts to dance to it, for this is kitchen music, after all. I take her hands and dance with her and I forget the writing as we weave together in and out of time.

It brings to mind the time Dillon Johnston and Guinn Batten took me to a festival in West Virginia, where this brilliant Old-time band played on the back of a lorry, and old folk and young folk got up and danced as the fancy took them: this big farmer of an old guy partnering a little girl about my Mary's age, making delicate, floaty triplet steps with his yellow-laced big red boots in counterpoint to her petite feet. I can still hear the cluck and gurgle of the banjo, the lovely, scrapy rosiny push of the fiddle, nice little bass runs on the guitar picking out significant bits of rhythm . . . ridge after ridge, the mountains stretch away into the blue distance, and the memory of the Blue Ridge Mountains of Virginia blurs into the present as I listen to the Iron Mountain String Band for about the eighteenth time. It is the fifteenth of May, 1995, and the Band is playing some time in 1992, as recorded in a studio in Galax, Virginia, but I hear it different every time.

Compared to the baroque plethora of the Irish repertoire, American Old-time has relatively few tunes. Sets or medleys of tunes are rarely played, but the one tune is played many times. The playing is relatively unadorned: most of the work on the fiddle, for example, is done by the bow (though the left hand can be very subtle, making little off-beat finger-flicks against the bow, to give the note an edge). Yet, given these restrictions, the music is never boring, because it defeats time. The world beyond the tune moves to a different time. I've just counted how many times the Iron Mountain String Band play 'Sugar Hill' on a six-minute-long track, and it comes to fourteen, which is really twenty-eight, since the tune is doubled. This is a lot of times; but in real life, no one's counting – you lose track of numbers. You have to move to the music and be taken over by its mantra. In its circular reiteration and reprises, 'Old-time' is a paradox: it is not old, but of the here-and-now; its players constantly renew the breakdowns which have stood the clichéd test of time.

Old-time is not Bluegrass, and I am often bored by Bluegrass precisely because of its striving for newness and effect, its fussy, jazzy virtuosity. In Bluegrass, everyone must get a break, and because the breaks are predicated they tend to make the tunes they've taken in sound all the same, as the soloist goes through his formulae of variations. I generalise, of course, for Old-time and Bluegrass are not diametrically opposed, but are different shades of a spectrum that runs all the way to Country and back again.

Take the case of Fiddlin' John Carson, who is often represented as the man who started the Country music boom; equally, he can be credited as being the progenitor of Bluegrass. I first heard of Carson when I was introduced to the American musician Kenny Hall, some twenty years ago in Dublin. 'You're Carson?' he says. 'You must be something to Fiddlin' John.' It's possible. John Carson (and I used to have a mad Uncle John) was born on 23 March 1868 on a farm in Fannin County, Georgia. When he was ten years old, he inherited the fiddle his grandfather had brought over from Ireland. As a young man, he moved to the Atlanta area and worked as a race-horse jockey, among other things. Though not working regularly as a musician at this time, he was already known as 'Fiddlin' John'. Here, as recorded in the *Radio Digest* of 7 November 1925, is how he got his name:

One of the most interesting memories in the vari-colored career of the Fannin County virtuoso is the fiddling contest at which the mountain boy outfiddled Governor Bob Taylor of Tennessee. This contest was the big event of the year. 'Fiddlin' Bob', as he was popularly known, was renowned for his skill on the fiddle, and few had ever been found who were near enough his level to make a competition interesting.

But on this momentous occasion, a new adversary was discovered. A hardy mountaineer was entered in the contest, who was the pride and hope of his friends who had come along with him to lend any moral support they could. The contest went on and it was a thrilling battle between the two favourites – Governor Bob Taylor, and the unknown mountaineer. Then the finish and young Carson was declared winner and thereafter became known as Fiddlin' John, while Governor Taylor was so delighted with the young fellow's playing that right there on the spot, he bestowed his fiddle on the proud victor.

Carson soon became well known in the Atlanta area, playing as warm-up for travelling circuses and medicine shows; his ability to draw a crowd also led him into associations with some of Georgia's most distinguished politicians, who hired him to play and sing home-made campaign songs. However, his first record was not made until he was fifty-five, in June 1923; the industry was still in its infancy, and tended to be directed at a more affluent audience than those who would want to hear this style of music.

When the Okeh company issued 'The Little Old Log Cabin in the Lane/The Old Hen Cackled and the Rooster's Going to Crow', it was an immediate hit, to the extent that Fiddlin' John declared he could nearly give up making moonshine. Others, equally successful, followed, and all in all he recorded some one hundred and fifty sides. What is interesting is the staggering diversity of the material. Fiddlin' John was promiscuous in his repertoire, which included old British ballads, blackface minstrel songs, Tin Pan Alley and Broadway hits, religious songs, blues ballads, Victorian parlour songs, songs written specially about topical events; he even recorded 'It's a Long Way to Tipperary'. And, of course, Old-time fiddle tunes, of which he was a master. What comes through in this *mélange* is Fiddlin' John's strength of personality and a directness and commitment of approach which could make any song his own.

In this, of course, he was not alone, for real folk singers never confined themselves to an academically-perceived 'folk' repertoire somehow fixed in amber, despite the depredations of the twentieth century: they sang what was in the air and adapted it to fit their own aesthetic. What unifies the material in Fiddlin' John's case is the impeccable phrasing, the underlying pulse in the grain of his voice going against the ostensible rhythm of the tune. At times he reminds me of the Northern Irish singer, the late Eddie Butcher; at others, the modern Country singer George Jones. I suspect Fiddlin' John could be all things to all men, and it is not surprising that he should be claimed by the followers of diverse genres. To me, he is old-time personified.

Fiddlin' John's first records were solo, with his own fiddle accompaniment; thereafter, he played with a band known as the Virginia Reelers, which included, among others, his daughter Rosa Lee, otherwise known as Moonshine Kate, and a fiddle-player called 'Bully' Brewer. The following exchange with 'Bully' takes place on 'OK 45448':

Bully: I'm the best fiddler that ever wobbled a bow.
John: I don't give a durn, I'm the best fiddler that ever jerked the hairs of a horse's tail across the belly of a cat.
Bully: Well, I'll play 'Old Hen Cackle'.
John: Turn your dog loose.
Bully plays
Bully: Well, what're you going to play, John?
John: I'm going to play the fiddle . . . that's a durn sight more than you've done.

Fiddlin' John Carson's success prompted other record companies to produce similar material, and it has been reckoned that some fifty thousand such records – 'Hillbilly', 'Country', 'Old-time', call it what you will – were issued, thus leaving an archive hardly matched by the efforts of serious field collectors. The companies, prompted by a purely commercial instinct, produced what local people wanted to hear, and rarely let their own preconceptions about music interfere: Fiddlin' John's producer, for example, thought his voice was 'pluperfect awful', but when he saw how the records sold, you may be sure he didn't arrange to have him take voice production lessons. In addition to the records, sheet music was produced to secure copyright and more dollars. Irene Spain, the stepdaughter of another OK artist, the Revd Andrew Jenkins, was hired to do the job on Fiddlin' John:

Fiddlin' John Carson's recording of 'You'll Never Miss Your Mother Until She's Gone' was the very first record I transcribed and 'I'm Glad My Wife's in Europe' was the second. Poor John couldn't make a record unless he was a little more than half drunk and he always had to have a 'jaw-breaker' – a candy ball about half as big as a golf ball – in his mouth and he would roll that around while singing. His words were so muddled up at times that we had to almost guess at what he was saying to get them on paper. Daddy (Jenkins) and my husband were both ministers and we were quite ashamed to be playing such records in our house for some of them were truly vulgar. But we would close the windows and doors and sit by the hours and sweat them out until we got them. Daddy, being blind, had a more sensitive ear than I, and he could understand words that I could not. So we worked together.

Such were the early days of the Country music business. When the Depression came, Fiddlin' John's music dropped out of favour and he hit hard times. However, when Eugene Talmadge, who knew Carson well, was elected Governor of Georgia, Fiddlin' John squatted in an elevator in the State Capitol and refused to budge until he got the job of running it. It reminds me of how the great *sean-nós* singer Joe Heaney worked as an epauletted doorman for a hotel just opposite the Dakota, where John Lennon was shot. The Governor saw to it that Fiddlin' John did get the job, and he worked there until a few weeks before his death on 11 December 1949. He was aged eighty-one. I was aged fourteen months. We live in each other's long shadows.

The Bush in the Tux

I never met The Shadow, but I heard these things about him.

No one I have asked is exactly sure why The Shadow was so-called. Some claim he shadowed the fiddle-player Sean McGuire. Others deny this; he was a fiddle-player in his own right. Some attribute it to his long thin height and his dapper, dude rancher style of dressing.

The Shadow painted a copy of the Sistine Chapel ceiling on his ceiling.

Some believed The Shadow just appeared, without having gone through the motions of getting there.

The Shadow was reputed to be the best hitch-hiker in Ireland. Dressed in cowboy hat and boots, a guitar case slung over one shoulder and a fiddle case slung over the other, he presented an intriguing figure to the passing traffic.

Often it was felt that the session lacked a certain *je ne sais quoi* without The Shadow's presence. People looked for him when he wasn't there.

It puts me in mind, somehow, of the late Mickey Golly of Glencolmcille, who I was told was a great fiddle-player. The only time I met him, in the Sliabh Liag Hotel in Carrick, he was playing 'air' or 'poteen' fiddle: playing with no fiddle and no bow. But the shapes he made convinced me.

The Shadow, according to one source, was also 'a very loud guitar-player and at times could be mistaken for a lightly played piano.'

The Shadow was invited to be present at the only meeting of the great fiddle-player John Doherty and the great box-player Joe Cooley. This took place in O'Beirne's Hotel in Carrick, and I'm trying to establish if this was, in fact, a former name for the Sliabh Liag. During lulls between tunes, The Shadow would take up his guitar and launch into his repertoire of cowboy songs. Among his favourites were 'The Yellow Rose of Texas' and 'The Red River Valley'. John Doherty was reputed to have been much taken by The Shadow's rendition of the American fiddle tunes, 'The Orange Blossom Special' and 'The Mocking Bird', and learned them then and there. The trio – Doherty, Cooley and The Shadow – played for three days and three nights, and each night was better than the last. The year was 1952.

The Shadow was the pseudonym of Sean McLoughlin of Armoy, County Antrim.

The Shadow's last request was to be buried with his boots on, wearing a white tuxedo with a half-bottle of Bushmills in the inside pocket.

The Ould Orange Flute

Ambiguous shadows loom behind us, the way our names are
predicated for us; and in Northern Ireland my name is perceived
as an oxymoron, the product of a mixed marriage. 'Ciaran', from
the Irish *ciar*, dark-haired, is about as Catholic as you can get.
There are some fourteen Ciarans in the calendar of saints, of
whom the most illustrious are Ciaran of Saighir and Ciaran of
Clonmacnoise. Both had a predeliction for the miraculous: Ciaran
of Saighir in particular, thought by some to be a contemporary
of Patrick and by others to be pre-Patrician, existed in that Tír
na n-Og (Land of Eternal Youth), between the pagan and the
Christian worlds, and went around raising the dead (the catch
being that they had to become monks and follow him) and striking
kings dumb for their insolence. 'Carson', on the other hand, is
perceived as an epitome of Protestant nomenclature, as embodied
in the person of Edward Carson. Revered as founder-father of the
state of Northern Ireland, Carson, according to folk rumour, was
really a Carsoni from Italian stock, which would account for the
aquiline Mussolini cast of his features; and, wearing his barrister's
wig, Carson successfully prosecuted Oscar Wilde, that paradoxical,
ambiguous, bent Irishman.

On Easter Sundays my paradoxical Catholic father William
Carson, or Liam Mac Carráin, as he defined himself in Gaelic
mode, would bring us children to the slopes of Stormont, seat of
the Northern Ireland parliament, where, presided over by the giant
bronze statue of Edward Carson, we would roll our eggs. Whether
this was a subversive act or one of reconciliation I cannot tell, but
its ambiguity mirrored that of the family history. My father and
mother met at Irish classes during the Second World War. She
was Mary Maginn, a daughter of the son of Finn, the ancient Irish

hero; my father maintained that he was really a McCarron, and his lineage had been Englishly corrupted into Carson. It was not until my wedding day* that he revealed in an off-hand conversational aside that his grandfather was a Protestant from Ballymena.

A cabinet-maker by trade, my great-grandfather had come to work in Belfast and turned Catholic when he met his Catholic wife. He married twice and fathered twenty-two children, and for a long time I had this ideal, symmetrically-garbled version of the saga in my mind, where two football teams of Prods and Taigs lined up against each other in a friendly fixture. In reality, his first wife died after giving birth to nine children, and he had thirteen by the second; all Catholic. He too was William Carson; but my father argued strongly for the possibility that his grandfather's father or father's father had turned from being Catholic, and was really a McCarron. Their Carson aspect was a mere blip in history.

Whatever the case, it made some kind of atavistic sense that, every Twelfth of July for years, my father would take us down Stockman's Lane from Catholic Andersonstown to the Protestant Lisburn Road to watch the Orangemen's parade – 'The Walk', as it was known – on its progress to 'The Field'. My brother next-to-me and I would climb the big billboard on the corner of the road: we could see for a mile, as accordioned waves of banners and regalia undulated slowly towards us in their glistening, heat-hazed, gold and purple cohorts, and the various drills of quick-stepping flute bands beat out their overlapping times, intertangled with the more majestic skirl of pipes and their synchronous regiments of waving kilts. The sounds advancing towards us were the future, yet each band marched in its continuous present, and as it passed where we stood, it defined itself to the exclusion of the others. Then they dwindled off into the past, the predetermined venue of The Field. In this context, I am reminded by the poet Michael Longley that the Ancient Greeks believed that the future was behind them, since facing forwards, they could only see the past.

Catholics, too, had their parades, as witnessed by the Ancient Order of Hibernians, but they had a minority appeal within the minority. 'The Hibs' marched as a mirror image of the Orange

---

* 16 October 1982. Interestingly, the nice eccentric priest wrote my name as 'Casson', and so it is on our marriage certificate. So, formally, Deirdre Shannon and I are probably not married at all.

Order, replete with banners and flute bands and drums. One side stole off the other, literally:

> Ah well, there was these Hibernians goin' along the road there, with this drum called 'Roarin' Meg', named for the cannon in Derry, an' there was this boy, Right McKnight, watchin' them walkin'. Him and he's Da had went up to hear it. He took a fancy to this drum, for she had the tone in her, an' the Hibernians when they were goin' along broke one of the heads, an' they came up to this woman Bridget Kelly's pub, an' they all went in for a drink, an' they left the drum, sayin' they'd call back for it again, after.
>
> Then when the Hibernians was away down the road, doesn't Right McKnight go to the door, an' say he was here to collect the drum, an' away he goes, off down the road with her. Now it bein' August, an' not that far off Harvest, McKnight hides the drum in the corn, an' he lies with her all night, an' the next day, on the train, an' away back to Belfast.
>
> An' he puts two new heads on her, an' scrapes her down, an' puts a cock on her, an' calls her 'The Cock of the North', an' away out to a match. But the Hibernians got the peelers on to this, an' the peelers got three of them to identify her, but McKnight had changed her so much, they couldn't tell her, an' she's there yet, only she fell apart about fifteen year ago.

> Robert McLeese, interviewed by
> Gary Hastings, April 1975

Stories such as this abound. One side is in the shadow of the other, regalia and paraphernalia reflected in each other's Polaroids. But we Catholics had another kind of parade, the religious procession, like those held in May to venerate the Virgin Mary. This differed from The Walk in that its space was not linear: beginning at the church, it proceeded to circumscribe the bounds of the parish, to end at the church again. It was the image of a rosary. Here, hymn-singing became an unconscious round, as there was a Chinese-whisper time lag between the head and tail of the procession, and the tail would still be singing while the head had by now embarked on a recital of the rosary.

The intention of the Marian procession was to make the parish a bulwark against the forces of evil; it was an assertion of territory, but an internalised one, presided over by the ultimate territorial claim of Heaven. The Orangemen's Field seems also to be concerned with territory, an externalised ideal space which represents Northern Ireland, or Ulster: for us children, it was a kind of paleface stockade, and we were Indians.

The Field at Finaghy (from the Irish *fionn achaidh*, fair field) lay about half a mile behind our semi-detached house, and, after watching The Walk in the morning we would go home, grab a bite to eat and set off across the border fields, skulking under hedges as we neared The Field. Here, speeches were made by way of crackly tannoy systems on shaky stages, people filed in and out of marquees, and courting couples sprawled in the long-grassed margins. We Catholics now pretended to be palefaces, as if we'd been stolen by the Indians as babies, and were Indian in mind but not in body. We walked around in fearful nonchalance, not knowing when we would be challenged, but we never were; we might as well have been invisible. We were scavengers, collecting empty beer and lemonade bottles that were later exchanged for cash; our eyes would light up at the glint of loose change fallen from drunken pockets. We were uninvited symbiotic guests, like involuntary crocodile birds; perhaps we were chameleons. It was fair exchange, as in the Lambeg mnemonic, 'I'll give ye thirty shillings for your one pound ten, your one pound ten . . .'

It is Easter 1984, the centennial of the Gaelic Athletic Association, and stolid delegates from the thirty-two counties are filing into the Whitla Hall at Queen's University for some commemorative business or other. As I pass by, I can hear the strains of a flute band just down the road, in Loyalist Sandy Row: the Junior Apprentice Boys are marching. The culture clash is, perhaps, not as extreme as it appears: the GAA, after all, are fond of marching bands; and the skeletons of many of the so-called 'Orange' tunes resemble those in the so-called 'Green' family cupboard. 'The Boyne Water' is precisely the same tune as '*Rosc Catha na Mumhan*' (The Battle-cry of Munster), alternatively known as '*Marchechaid na*

Buinne'*. Tunes, of themselves, have no ideological message, and what constitutes a 'party' tune depends on verbal labels and the perception of the hearer:

> *Are the tunes always, or even generally, party tunes?*

I do not think they are; they sometimes play what are called party tunes, but in fact it is hard to know what a party tune is.

> *Is 'The Boyne Water' a party tune?*

That is hard to give an answer to, because 'The Boyne Water', as I have heard, was a Jacobite tune composed by a Roman Catholic, whether as King James' march, or a lamentation after it, I am not exactly certain, but from the Irish of it, I should say it was The March of the Boyne.

> *What is the Irish of it?*

'*Marchechaid na Buinne*', signifying the cavalcade of the Boyne.

> *Is 'Croppies Lie Down' a party tune?*

I do not consider it so, because I think any person that would take offence at it as a party tune, must have identified himself with the rebels who went by the name of Croppies.

> *What is your opinion as to 'Patrick's Day', and 'The White Cockade'?*

'Patrick's Day' is a tune that has regularly been looked upon as a party tune by the Protestants, taken up in that way, and it is a very foolish thing on all sides, I think, attaching as much importance to tunes; but 'Patrick's Day' is certainly considered by Protestants in my country as a party tune upon the one side, and a party tune upon the other. I remember that when Louis XVIII was restored, 'The White Cockade' was played by the people who were friendly to him; I remember 'God Save the King' being made a violent party tune.

---

* A garbled spelling, Nicholas Carolan informs me.

You know that in Dublin Theatre, 'God Save the King' is played and if anyone does not take off his hat, some loyal person is found to assist him?

Yes, I have heard that. In 1797 they sang in Belfast, 'God save the Guillotine, that beheaded both King and Queen'.

> from *Report from the Select Committee Appointed to Inquire into: The Nature, Character, Extent and Tendency of Orange Lodges, Associations or Societies in Ireland,* House of Commons, 1835

Back in 1984, I'd bought a B flat band flute. I lift it up again in 1995 and try my hand at the 'Orange' tunes that were going around in my head back then, as they are now, half-memorised from years before I ever set hands on a flute. My fingers, used to the Sligo-Leitrim style of playing I've adopted (or that adopted me), keep putting in unnecessary frills: I discover again the difficulty of what seems simple. Part of me likes this 'Kick the Pope' music for its jaunty freedom from respectability. I like its energy and fire, even though the fire might be directed against me, or, rather, a perception of what I might be, a Ciaran rather than a Carson. Trying to play these tunes reminds me of trying to play Kerry polkas, some of which, it is said, came from the repertoire of military bands in Southern garrison towns. Their pulse inclines against the norm, whatever the 'norm' is. They turn a different way; they put me in mind of other turns, or turnings, such as that of my great-grandfather William Carson, who was a kind of Bob Williamson:

> In the County Tyrone, near the town of Dungannon,
> Where many's the ruction myself had a han' in,
> Bob Williamson lived, a weaver by trade
> And all of us thought him a stout Orange blade.
> On the Twelfth of July as it yearly did come
> Bob played on his flute to the sound of the drum;
> You may talk of your harp, your piano or lute,
> But there's nothing compared to the ould Orange flute.
>
> But Bob the deceiver he took us all in,
> For he married a Papish called Brigid McGinn,

Turned Papish himself, and forsook the old cause
That gave us our freedom, religion and laws.
Now the boys of the place made some comment upon it
And Bob had to flee to the province of Connaught.
He fled with his wife and his fixings to boot
And along with the latter his ould Orange flute.

At the chapel on Sundays to atone for past deeds
He said *Paters* and *Aves* and counted his beads,
Till after some time, at the priest's own desire
He went with his flute for to play in the choir.
He went with his ould flute to play in the Mass,
And the instrument shivered, and sighed, O alas!
And blow as he would, though it made a great noise,
The flute would play only 'The Protestant Boys'.

Bob jumped, and he started, and got in a flutter,
And threw his ould flute in the blest Holy Water;
He thought that this charm would bring some other sound;
When he blew it again, it played 'Croppies Lie Down'.
And for all he could finger and whistle and blow,
To play Papish music he found it no go.
'Kick the Pope', 'The Boyne Water', it freely would sound,
But one Papish squeak in it couldn't be found.

At a council of priests that was held the next day,
They decided to banish the ould flute away.
For they couldn't knock heresy out of its head
So they bought Bob a new one to play in its stead.
Well, the ould flute was doomed and its fate was pathetic,
'Twas fastened and burned at the stake as heretic.
As the flames roared around it they heard a quare noise,
'Twas the ould flute still whistling 'The Protestant Boys'.

Naturally, this song reminds me of my father, too. He was
a postman, and for a while his round, or 'walk' as it was
known in the trade, took in part of the Protestant Shankill
Road. One eleventh of July he was invited into a house to
have a bottle of stout to celebrate the forthcoming glorious
occasion. At the drop of a hat he sang 'The Ould Orange

Flute'. He sang 'The Orange Lily'. It was a hot day, and on the verge of launching into 'Dolly's Brae', he pulled out his pocket-handkerchief to wipe his brow, whereupon his rosary beads fell out and clattered to the floor, and Willie Carson was exposed as Liam Mac Carráin.*

Before the flutes, there were fifes, still played widely in parts of the USA, that remind me of Marianne Moore's poem 'The Steeple-Jack', where 'The/whirlwind fife-and-drum of the storm bends the salt/marsh grass, disturbs stars in the sky and the/star on the steeple' and 'it is a privilege to see so/much confusion'. I am also reminded of Captain Francis O'Neill, General Superintendent of the Chicago Police. The frontispiece portrait in his 1903 edition of *The Music of Ireland* shows him as sober, serious, moustachioed, and his embroidered Captain's cap is like my father's postman's cap with its authoritative black peak. Policeman, flute-player; which was the greater privilege?

The full-rigged ship *Minnehaha*, of Boston, on which I served 'before the mast', was wrecked on Baker's Island, in the mid-Pacific. Our crew, numbering twenty-eight, were taken off this coral islet after eleven days of Robinson Crusoe experiences by the brig *Zoe*, manned by a white captain and a Kanaka crew. Rations were necessarily limited almost to starvation. One of the Kanakas had a fine flute, on which he played a simple one-strain hymn with conscious pride almost every evening. Of course, this chance to show what could be done on the instrument was not to be overlooked. The result was most gratifying. As in the case of the Arkansaw traveller, there was nothing too good for me. My dusky brother cheerfully shared his *poi* and canned salmon with me thereafter. When we arrived at Honolulu, the capital of the Hawaiian Islands, after a voyage of thirty-four days, all but three of the castaways were sent to the Marine Hospital. I

---

* After I wrote this, I checked the story out with my father. His (presumably more authoritative) version differs from mine in some nice details: it was the actual Twelfth, not the eleventh, because postal deliveries did not stop for holidays, back then; the stout was Caffrey's; he spilled a little of the second bottle on his shirt, and then took out his handkerchief, whereupon the beads were spilled. My brother Pat has another version in which the man of the house excused himself, then went upstairs and came down brandishing a ceremonial Orange sword; this sounds like embroidery.

was one of the three robust ones, thanks to my musical friend, and was therefore sent straight to San Francisco. What became of my wrecked companions was never learned; but it can be seen how the trivial circumstance of a little musical skill exercised such an important influence on my future career.

Francis O'Neill, *Irish Folk Music:*
A Fascinating Hobby

Alternative universes loom before us with their many shadows.

Chief O'Neill's Favourites

'Francis O'Neill was born 25 August 1849, at Tralibane, three miles from Bantry, County Cork, Ireland, a district which has given birth to many Irishmen now prominent before the world, among whom may be mentioned A.M. Sullivan, T.D. Sullivan, the author of "God Save Ireland", and Tim Healy, MP. He was the son of John and Catherine (O'Mahoney) O'Neill, his father being an educated and well-to-do farmer, while his mother was one of the O'Mahoneys of Castle Mahon, now Castle Bernard, in the province of Munster. Her father, Donald Mor O'Mahoney, a man famous for his gigantic stature, was a latter day chieftain, and his grandson recalls seeing horse pistols, pikes and bayonets in abundance at his home near Drimaleague.

'Francis O'Neill found in the national school of Bantry a thoroughly sound education on all general subjects, including the classics. He was a bright boy, an omnivorous reader, an ardent student, and so distinguished himself in mathematics as to be named by his teacher "Philosopher O'Neill". At the age of fourteen he became senior monitor and later taught school. His elder brother's persistence, however, in appropriating his salary for investment in stock and cattle dealing, a course later well justified since he made a rapid fortune, to which was coupled an unquestionable desire for travel, led him when barely sixteen, and with the limited capital of five dollars, to start out in the world.

'His first two weeks producing no tangible result, he had an interview with Bishop Delaney of Cork, who proposed either to make of him a Christian Brother or a teacher in one of the Catholic schools. The losing his way and the consequent failure to keep an appointment with the bishop he now considers responsible for his failure to become a monk. This was in March, 1865, and the travel instinct being strong he worked his passage to Sunderland, in the north of England, and after various vicissitudes shipped there as a cabin boy, sailing up the Mediterranean and via the Dardanelles, the Bosphorus and the Black Sea to Odessa, the great southern port of Russia. On the return voyage, when landing in Sunderland harbor, an accident threw him off the vessel to the ground and he fractured his skull.

'A practiced swimmer, on starting for his next voyage to Alexandria, Egypt, where he remained nine weeks, he managed to save the boatswain's life in the Yarmouth Roads, in return for which he was brutally ill-treated during the whole voyage. After other voyages in which he had some very interesting eastern experiences, in July, 1866, he shipped at Liverpool on the packet ship *Emerald Isle*, and five weeks later landed in New York. Santa Cruz, West Indies, was next visited, and many other places in South America.

'Later he shipped at New York on the *Minnehaha* of Boston, bound for Japan, where he arrived after a voyage lasting seven months and full also of interesting and exciting experiences. Ten weeks were spent there and then the journey was continued to Honolulu and he spent an interesting five weeks in that land of earthquakes. Back to San Francisco, Mr O'Neill determined to try a new experience and see the country, so hired himself to take charge of a flock of sheep. Five months in the Sierra Nevada Mountains were so passed, and then a return was made to New York, via Cape Horn, after a few weeks' stay at Culiacan on the west of Mexico.

'Having travelled for years by land and sea all over the globe, and circumnavigating the globe before attaining his majority, a few hundred dollars having been saved by him, he came westwards with the intention of buying and establishing a home. Edina, in Knox County, Missouri, was selected, and having passed the necessary examination successfully, he obtained employment teaching in the district school during the winter of 1869 . . .

'The year 1871 saw a return to Chicago, and Mr O'Neill found employment with the Chicago & Alton Railroad, as laborer in the freight house. A few weeks afterwards he became check clerk and then other promotions until he was given complete charge of the lumber business on the south branch. The work was heavy and the remuneration so deplorably small that he decided to try for a position on the police force. He received his appointment under Elmer Washburne and was sworn in July 12th, 1873, being assigned to Harrison Street Station under Captain Buckley. The following month he was shot in an encounter with a notorious burglar and still carries a memento in a bullet encysted near the spine. For his bravery the following day he was advanced to be regular patrolman by the unanimous vote of the police board.

'In August, 1878, he was made desk sergeant and transferred to Deering Street Station. Chief of Police Austin J. Doyle moved him in 1884 to the general superintendent's office and advanced to patrol sergeant January 1st, 1887. Raised to lieutenant exactly three years later, he continued in various confidential positions in the general superintendent's office. On his own request Chief of Police Major R.W. McClaughry transferred him to the Tenth Precinct at Hyde Park, where he remained until recalled to Harrison Street Station by Chief of Police Brennan in July, 1893. The following month the latter made him his private secretary, and April 17th, 1894 he was promoted to captain and assigned in charge of the Eighth District, the Union Stock Yards. Here he succeeded in adding additional laurels to his already excellent record.

'In July, 1894, when the railroad riots were at their height his district was the center of the strike trouble, and here he was personally in charge. His assistants were brave and well-tried officers, but his was the chief responsibility of withstanding the attack of five thousand men thoroughly enraged by the state militia's action. His courage and determination undoubtedly prevented the most serious consequences and forced the unthinking mob to understand that in Chicago law and order were at all times and under all circumstances superior to lawlessness, riot, and vandalism . . .

'This record has increased year after year, and to-day he bears the reputation that there is in the police service no more capable, efficient or braver officer. While in his manner he is unassuming, even to a degree of shyness, when there is any call of duty his performance is immediate and perfect . . .

'He is the only member in Chicago of the Cork Historical and Archaeological Society, which he joined on its organization in 1891, and of which his boyhood playmate at Bantry, the Right Reverend Richard A. Sheehan, bishop of Waterford and Lismore, is the first president. He belongs to no secret societies, but is a member of the Police Benevolent Association . . .

'Being possessed of a keen business instinct, he has made a number of exceedingly profitable real estate investments which have assured him a good income and made the latter years of a peculiarly adventurous life and a most interesting career, one of such peaceful and happy days as his kindly character and eminent good parts unquestionably deserve.'

Charles French, *The Biographical History of the American Irish in Chicago*, 1898

Back in the Sixties, before I knew better, I associated the name of the then popular hornpipe, 'Chief O'Neill's Favourite', with some class of a Gaelic lord. The paradoxical reality is better. As the eponymous Chief of Police in Chicago, O'Neill was in a unique position to indulge his 'fascinating hobby', recruiting itinerant musicians into the Force and setting out to collect music from the large immigrant Irish population, which included practitioners from most regions in Ireland. The town must have been bursting with tunes, as were the corridors of power:

> One Monday morning I unexpectedly encountered John McFadden in the corridor outside my office door in the City Hall, and wondering what could have happened since we parted the evening before, I asked, 'What brings you here so early, John?' 'I want to see you privately in your office, Chief,' he quietly replied. To my suggestion that we could transact our business just as well where we were as in my office, where so many were waiting, he did not agree, so in we went through three intervening rooms. When the door was closed behind us Mac did not keep me long in suspense. 'Chief, I lost the third part of 'Paddy in London' which you gave me last night. I had it all when going to bed, but when I got up this morning, all I could remember were the first and second parts, and I want you to whistle the missing part for me again.'
> When he had left he had it all once more, and he never forgot it either, for it is one of his favorite tunes which is most admired.

And O'Neill's tenacity in 'getting his man' is nicely illustrated by the following anecdote:

A few months had passed pleasantly for all concerned, when there came to Chicago, Power's delightful Irish play, *The Ivy Leaf*. Their piper, Eddie Joyce, a brilliant young musician, took sick and was sent to a hospital. Great failings are not infrequently the concomitants of great talents, and so this precocious genius, whose fame was nation-wide, passed away in his teens, sincerely mourned by a large circle of admirers. To take his place temporarily, Delaney reluctantly consented; but such were his success and popularity, that Powers insisted on keeping him permanently on an increased salary. While we could not help congratulating Delaney, we were by no means reconciled to our loss. Nothing but a more desirable position in Chicago could be expected to allure him to return. When that had been arranged for, the writer intercepted *The Ivy Leaf* company in New York city and returned to the western metropolis, accompanied by our piper, where he became and still is a member of the Chicago police force. The interest in the study and practice of traditional Irish Music was noticeably affected by the excellence of Delaney's execution, for he was in great demand as an attraction on festive and various public occasions.

As for collecting music rather than musicians, O'Neill was immensely more equipped than the likes of the academically respectable Petrie, Joyce and Bunting, whose classical training and antiquarian bent led them to 'arrange' the music to conform to conventional European tonalities and harmonies. Illiterate in music, he had a phenomenal musical memory. He came to the music as a traditional musician; he did not impose a foreign character on it, since he was a native.

O'Neill worked in tandem with his namesake Sergeant James O'Neill, a trained musician from County Down who would transcribe the tunes from his Chief's lilting, whistling or playing. It began as a hobbyistic enterprise, but gradually became a major work, culminating in the publication of *O'Neill's Music of Ireland* in 1903. This was followed, in 1907, by an edition containing only the dance music, *The Dance Music of Ireland: A Thousand Gems*. It proved a popular success and became a reference point for Irish traditional musicians everywhere: to this day, if someone asks if a tune is 'in the book', they mean *The Dance Music of Ireland*. In this context, the expression being 'booked' takes on a whole new meaning; and the present writer would give a lot to be booked into this Chicago cop-shop:

> Many an impromptu concert in which the writer took part enlivened the old Deering Street Police Station about this time. A unique substitute for a drum was operated by Patrolman Michael Keating, who, forcing a broomstick handle held rigidly against the maple floor at a certain angle, gave a passable imitation of a kettle-drum. His ingenuity and execution never failed to evoke liberal applause.

Trying to imagine myself there, I recall the missing third part of the tune, thanks to O'Neill; and recognise the response of 'a celebrated exile', Patrick O'Leary of Adelaide, South Australia, quoted proudly by O'Neill in his introduction to *The Dance Music of Ireland*:

> For over a third of a century I have been waiting, watching, hoping and praying, that God might inspire some Irishman, or association of Irishmen, to collect and publish just such a work as *The Dance Music of Ireland* – the grand old music – the weird, beautiful, wild and mournful reel tunes that entranced me when a child, a youth, a man, in the street or barn, at the bonfire or on the hill-top; the music, the never-to-be-forgotten strains that often made my blood alternately freeze or flame – that made me when a child, sitting beneath the fiddler's chair, weep with delight or sadness, a condition of mind impossible to describe. Many of the grand old tunes learned from the lips of my poor dead mother which I had not heard since childhood, and still others that I had heard played when a boy, were floating about in my memory, disconnected and fragmentary, before your book came. Well, dear sir, I thank God that I have lived to see my dreams fully realized, and my prayer answered more fully than my wildest ambition had dared to go.

Good Morning to Your Nightcap

We are always looking for the missing part of the tune; and all we've ever heard is in there somewhere, all we've witnessed, buried in the memory. Insert an electrode into the limbic system of the brain and an area of your life you thought you'd never occupied till then will light up: you will feel a salt tang on your lips as your four-year-old toes curl against the ridged-sand-ache beneath your instep and the cool skim water that you stand in. Isolated on the huge blinding strand, you get a whiff of turf and ozone. So I have heard it described, the present cancelled by a past reality.

At the same time I see a dimpled, pockmarked, sunshine-whitewashed, dazzling gable wall that is a bumpy map of the reality I temporarily inhabit. I see a microscopic me wandering across it, pleasurably lost in its terrain. The world is the size of a gable wall and the room on the other side of it is an antechamber to the universe. As I visualise musicians sitting in it, playing in the kitchen, their moving shadows on the inside wall flicker and loom like hieroglyphic deities: they are ensconced amid the constellations of the Irish diaspora, negotiating it and all its interlayered sidereal times.

Or, listening to the Cooley LP yet again, and wanting to be present at the *ceili*, I imagine myself to be a ghost from the future, that has crawled through the wired cracks of intervening times and emerged from the light-socket to flit across the dancers and musicians like a strobe.

Music defeats time by its mnemonic. Every day, tunes float into my head unbidden; I am caught up in their ingrained patterns. The tune is not a story, but stories cling to it; it is a rolling stone that gathers moss. Thinking of 'Good Morning to Your Nightcap', for example, I cannot help but think of Séamus Ennis because I half-remember some garbled story of his playing it or naming it in response to the supposed last jar of an early-morning session; I can hear the slow aplomb of his voice talking in inverted commas. The title is a mannerly corrective, in which Ennis subverts or puts down time. I see Ennis playing: visualising his long bony fingers on the chanter, I remark how like Joe Burke's they are, negotiating dance-step patterns on the keyboard.

I am drawn towards a memory of Joe Burke telling me about visiting Cooley on his death-bed. I see Joe Cooley, whom I never met, with that jaunty deadly cigarette between his lips, and hear him playing 'Last Night's Fun'. I do not know how many times I've heard the tune; I do not know how many times I've played it. I have played it on sunlit street corners; in small hotels in the small hours; I've lilted it in kitchens and in halls; I've whistled it along the road or in the bath. I've played it with many people, people I knew and people I'd just met. It's been played countless times by others; many feet have moved to it in different times.

As we apprehend the tune, we enter in and out of time, and mark its various times. Through the contoured haze of smoke and buzz of conversation, we perceive a girl's voice saying for the *nth* time, 'I haven't seen him dancing in years'.

The ghosts of voices circulate in grooves of dust. Everything is a black gloss: corrigenda and addenda, a thousand couples reeling in a palimpsest of dance-step patterns, as their feet step past the foot-notes.